The Work of Charles Samuel Keene

Charles Samuel Keene (1823–1891). Portrait photograph with overcoat and hat, probably by H. Harral, *c.* 1865.

The Work of
Charles Samuel Keene

Simon Houfe

SCOLAR PRESS

Published by
SCOLAR PRESS
Gower House
Croft Road
Aldershot
Hants GU11 3HR
England

Ashgate Publishing Company
Old Post Road
Brookfield
Vermont 05036–9704
USA

British Library Cataloguing-in-Publication data

Houfe, Simon
   Work of Charles Samuel Keene
   I. Title
   741.6092

Library of Congress Cataloging-in-Publication Data

Houfe, Simon
      The work of Charles Samuel Keene / Simon Houfe.
         p.   cm.
      Includes bibliographical references and index.
      ISBN 0–85967–986–1 (hardback)
      1. Keene, Charles, 1823–1891—Criticism and interpretation.
   I. Keene, Charles, 1823–1891. II. Title.
   NE2115.K4H68 1995
   780'.092—dc20   95–11681
                  CIP

ISBN 0 85967 986 1

Typeset in Plantin by Bournemouth Colour Press and printed in Great Britain by the University Press Cambridge

Contents

Illustrations

Introduction

In 1986, Michael Broadbent of Christie's, a renowned collector of Charles Keene's work, asked me if I would collaborate with him on a centenary exhibition to mark the year of Keene's death. It was a wonderful opportunity for me to indulge my passion for the artist's drawings that had developed when I was working at the Victoria and Albert Museum in the 1960s. The result was the comprehensive exhibition, mounted at Christie's between December 1990 and January 1991, for which I wrote a catalogue and helped in the choice of exhibits. Largely due to Michael Broadbent's expertise, the show included a notable selection of Keene's work and received very extensive coverage in the art press.

Despite its success in London and in the smaller exhibition of the Broadbent Collection shown at Ipswich, I still felt that there was more to tell of this remarkable Victorian figure. The beautifully produced exhibition catalogue could not go into detail on many of Keene's works nor was there time to carry out extensive new research. Public viewing produced some fascinating discoveries including a hitherto unknown photograph of the artist and at least two new portraits, one a self-portrait in oils. It seemed to me important to take this fresh growth of interest in Keene a step further and produce a short book on his life and drawings.

Anyone undertaking this task must be very well aware of the great names who have gone down this path previously. George Somes Layard, the historian of so much to do with Victorian illustration, published his monumental *Life and Letters of Charles Keene of 'Punch'* in 1892. It remains a very important quarry of informed comment about the artist, although its chapters are rambling and not chronological. In 1897, Joseph Pennell produced his large folio *The Work of Charles Keene* which remains a landmark for those interested in the draughtsmanship alone. It has a valuable bibliography and a catalogue of the etched work compiled by W.H. Chesson. It says much for Keene's standing that two such professional books should have been published within six years of his death. Further works were to follow early in the century: the complete etched work with an introduction by M.H. Spielmann (1903), and *Charles Keene: The Artists' Artist* by Sir Lionel Lindsay (1934). More specialist studies were *Charles*

Keene, Etcher, Draughtsman and Illustrator by Frank L. Emanuel (1932) and an article in the *Print Collector's Quarterly* for 1930. It could be said that Keene never totally went out of fashion even when Victorian art was at its nadir.

The most recent work to cover new ground was Derek Hudson's pioneering study *Charles Keene* (1947), which illustrated many subjects for the first time and analysed Keene's stylistic development and technique in a more professional manner. This remained the most considerable study for forty years, although the Arts Council organised an exhibition in 1952 for which Lord Clark wrote the introduction. During the early 1950s the Lowinsky and Emanuel collections came on the market, so that there was fresh interest aroused and new discoveries to be made.

The 1980s can now be seen as a time when interest in British illustration was revived and some of its famous artists were revalued. The black and white work of the *Punch* men, long neglected by art historians, was suddenly seen to be a significant contribution by this country to the European tradition. Regular sales of illustrative work began to be held and several important dealers devoted a large part of their exhibition space to this field. This new burst of interest also generated an appreciation of contemporary book illustrators whose originality and inventiveness tended to be overlooked. All of this would have been appreciated by admirers and collectors of Keene; they recognise that in him they have an illustrator of international importance and the only one (apart from Beardsley) to have reached a European stage.

Keene was very dear to the heart of the Victorians, but associated in their minds with *Punch* and humour. When Bradbury & Agnew produced their 'Copyright Edition' of *Mrs Caudle's Curtain Lectures* in 1888, they illustrated it with both the Leech and the Keene wood engravings crammed together on the pages. The effect was to make the two great artists of the journal inseparable. With hindsight we can see that they were very different and that Keene must be assessed as a formidable black and white artist in his own right, apart from the magazine that gave him his opportunities.

In gathering together the Keene drawings for this volume, I have tried to show his varying styles of draughtsmanship. With this in mind I have not included the joke legends below the drawings, partly because few of them are particularly funny and partly because I wish to concentrate on the art of Keene.

Simon Houfe

Acknowledgements

It would have been impossible to contemplate this book without the help and advice of notable collectors of Keene's work. I would mention in particular Michael Broadbent, whose collection of drawings, prints and memorabilia is unrivalled in this field. I was extremely fortunate to meet Michael Cook who owns an important group of pen drawings and he generously allowed me to reproduce fourteen of them in this volume. Cyril Fry allowed me to examine the Crawhall album in his possession and to use illustrations from it as well as correspondence between Keene and J.C. Barnes. Dr Fry kindly gave me permission to reproduce his sketch of musicians.

Mrs Jeanne Wilkins kindly showed me the papers of her grandfather Sir F.G. Burnand; Amanda Jane Doran of the *Punch* Library pointed me in the direction of interesting sources, and Paul Goldman and John Christian gave me valuable advice. Chris Beetles of Beetles Gallery, Ryder Street, St James's, let me examine his portfolios of Keene drawings and gave me permission to use them here. I also received help at various times from David Wootton, Bill Drummond and Rodney Engen, when he was on the staff of Maas Gallery.

During the time that I was researching I had great help from the staff of the London Library, the Cambridge University Library and the Art Library of the Fitzwilliam Museum, Cambridge. The British Museum kindly allowed me to reproduce their fine drawing of a studio and the Syndics of the Fitzwilliam Museum, Cambridge, and the Visitors of the Ashmolean Museum, Oxford gave me permission to use drawings from their collections. The Trustees of the Tate Gallery allowed me to publish three drawings from the Keene family collection bequeathed to the gallery and their fine study of artists in a studio recently acquired.

For DEREK HUDSON
A Pioneer in the Study of Charles Keene

1 The background of an artist

Chelsea in the 1860s must have been a place of enchantment. A sprawling riverside village with the character of a town, its distinctive history was marked by the grand groupings of Wren's Royal Hospital and the houses of Cheyne Row, while its spread of gardens, orchards and stretches of now-lost countryside still preserved its rural feeling. Ranelagh Gardens, the fashionable meeting place of the Georgian *beau monde* was still within living memory; Cremorne Gardens at the end of the King's Road was still a park of pleasure from which fireworks could be watched and the ascent of balloons witnessed. This area of contrasts where the town met the country and both met the river, had always had a particular attraction for artists. Paul Sandby had painted its riverbank and famous wooden water tower; Turner escaped to Chelsea where he enjoyed the anonymity of a tiny house and was known to the locals as the 'Admiral' or 'Admiral Booth'. By the middle of the nineteenth century it had developed a distinctive community of artists and writers, who appreciated the informality of the place, its raffish grandeur and its indigenous population of traders and river folk.

A well-known denizen of the Chelsea lanes and alleys at this time was a tall spare figure of rather shabby appearance. Approaching middle age, this gaunt character with a bony face, tufty beard and bright eyes could be seen striding to his work in the West End early in the morning and returning late in the afternoon. He never dressed in the conventional clothes of a gentleman and scholar although he was both, but always in the loose-fitting jacket, corduroys and billycock of the countryman, often with a knapsack slung over his shoulder. This was the rather eccentric appearance of Charles Keene, master draughtsman, talented etcher, musician, antiquary and letter-writer, going about his business in the bohemian milieu of Chelsea.

Keene had recently introduced Whistler to the locality and was on a nodding acquaintance with Rossetti; a habitué of the Chelsea waterfront, he was never to make the reaches of the Thames his own as Whistler and Rossetti did or as Walter Sickert and Walter Greaves were to do. Keene imbibed the spirit of the place as is evident in his drawings of its people, the ladies at doorways, the tradesmen with their carts, the boat-race crowds (see Plate 3.8, p.53), all immortalised in the pages of *Punch*.

Over a period of some forty years, Keene gained a reputation far outside the pages of the magazines; his genius was acknowledged by international artists, leading impressionists and the greatest writers of the age, but he still continued this unassuming life in two or three scruffy studios and lodgings in and around the King's Road.

Charles Keene's residences may have been in Chelsea, but his spiritual home was seventy miles away in Suffolk, the coastline of estuaries, rivulets and dunes where his ancestors had lived for hundreds of years. Although his livelihood as an artist was always to be made in London, his stays there were interspersed by long sojourns in the county of Suffolk, as if he needed to breathe its air and rekindle his creative powers in its familiar surroundings.

Charles Samuel Keene was born at Duval's Lane, Hornsey, on 10 August 1823, the son of Samuel Browne Keene, a solicitor and his wife Mary Sparrow. The Keene family must have originally been prosperous, for Samuel Browne Keene had been educated at Eton College before practising at Furnival's Inn. His early death in 1838, leaving a widow and five children, meant that the influence on the young artist came mostly from his mother's side in his formative years.

The Sparrows or Sparrowes of Ipswich were a force to be reckoned with – they had inhabited Sparrow's House in the Butter Market, the quintessential piece of East Anglian black-and-white architecture still standing today, for nearly three hundred years. Mrs Mary Keene must have been immensely proud of her ancestry and perhaps for this reason looms particularly large in the presence of her family. Before Mr Keene's death the family lived in Great Coram Street, the thoroughfare immortalised by Thackeray as the abode of prosperous tradesmen, while the young Charles was sent to a dame school in Bayswater. A little before 1838 the family moved to Ipswich so that Charles Samuel and his younger brother Henry Eddowes Keene could be educated at the Grammar School in Foundation Street, housed in the ancient refectory of the monks of the Blackfriars.

Perhaps this remarkable setting and the old Sparrow's house where he lodged with his mother, gave Keene his lifelong love of the past and antiquities. Sparrow's House was full of family portraits and had the added attraction of a secret chamber revealed behind sliding panels. The family were bookish and cultured, an uncle, William Sparrow, was an artist and the topographical draughtsman Samuel Read of Ipswich (1815–83) was a frequent visitor to the house. Suffolk was already established as an important stimulus to the artistic life. Two of its sons, Thomas Gainsborough and John Constable had become famous, and lesser artists formed a fledgling Suffolk School in the mid-nineteenth century. Thomas Churchyard (1798–1865) had made a name for himself in the Woodbridge region; E.R. Smythe (1810–99) and John Moore (1820–1902) were to follow. All these painters, like Gainsborough and Constable before them, were landscape painters and the depiction of these great sweeping farmlands with their vast skies seems to have been in the blood. It was also in the blood of Charles Keene, for though he was to be chiefly concerned with cities and people, he was a masterly landscapist and was above all a painter of natural things. His observation of the detail of a basket carried by an itinerant trader or the smock worn by a countryman was to have that same heightened reality that the earlier artists might have bestowed on a valley or a woodland.

Samuel Read has left us a pencil study of the young schoolboy Keene at the age of nine, a delicate, questioning, sensitive face with rather soulful eyes.[1] Contemporaries already noted that the young Keene 'affected the little refinements and courtesies of society, which derived from a graceful and highly cultivated mother'.[2] This is not to say that he was a mother's pet; there is a tradition at the school of a famous fight between Keene and another boy and he clearly enjoyed his time there. In later years he used his school experiences for drawings and even while attending the classes he decorated his Latin grammars with delightful little sketches (some were exhibited at the 1990 exhibition). Although they left a very deep impression on the young boy, the Ipswich years were very short, from about 1836 to 1839, by the autumn of 1839 the widowed Mrs Keene was back in London with her family.

The gangling youth that Charles Keene had become was steady, full of fun, but not easy to settle in any occupation. He was first placed in the office of his late father in Furnival's Inn in 1840 but this was not a success, his sensible mother shortly afterwards moving him to the office of William Pilkington (178?–1848) the architect. Although the work was more congenial, it still did not suit the restless spirit and the questing eye of the young Keene, whose outlet obviously had to be in a more demonstrative area of the arts. He was using his spare time to draw figure subjects based on history and romance, but was too self-effacing to procure any pecuniary gain from them. It was once again Mrs Keene who took them to Paternoster Row and finding a purchaser, kept her son supplied with a small stream of modest commissions. It was at this dealer's that Keene's work first came to the notice of the Whymper Brothers, wood-engravers of Lambeth. This firm had made its mark as the engravers for Charles Knight's voluminous *Arabian Nights Entertainments*, 1839 and on the other Knight enterprises, *Pictorial Shakespeare* and the *Penny Magazine*. These were not fine art but popular publishing, but they were in the vanguard of the new illustrated press.

The Whympers must have been impressed by the young man's work, but much more interested when they heard that Keene came from their own home town of Ipswich. Time and time again throughout his career, he was to encounter Suffolk men and to benefit from his Suffolk blood and origins. The Whympers were among the three most celebrated wood-engraving ateliers of the time, a forcing house for the apprentices who could find their way up the ladder from facsimile wood engraver to fully-fledged illustrator and, in some cases, fully-fledged painter.

Keene was apprenticed to them for five years, and although the tedium of the work must have been difficult for the young man, he developed a craftsmanship, discipline and attitude to his art that were to stand him in good stead. Keene's evenings were spent at the theatre, satisfying his great love of costume drama and historical romance; in the day, he sifted through the old books and prints of curiosity shops. An early letter of 1842 shows that he was already aware of his fellow illustrators and an admirer of the rising star among them John Leech (1817–1864). Leech, who was making his début in the recently founded *Punch*, was moving public taste towards the comedy of manners and away from the excesses of Georgian humour.

During the first part of his apprenticeship, Keene continued to live with his family, but from 1843 to 1845 he shared rooms in Great Ormond Street with George Ingelow, the brother of the poetess Jean Ingelow, also an Ipswich connection. From 1845, when his apprenticeship ended, Keene embarked on a bachelor life in rented rooms – this was to be the pattern for the next forty years. He rented a dilapidated attic studio above the Strand, a place of retreat and intense work, whose odd corners feature in many of his early drawings.

Henry Silver of *Punch* described the place when he first visited it in about 1850:

> This served him for a studio and museum of quaint properties; and here he chiefly used to sit, amid a chaos of old costumes, armour, proof-sheets, books and crockery and all manner of artistic waifs and strays and odds and ends, with a battered old lay figure for his personal companionship.[3]

All his early visitors – Henry Silver, Joseph Swain the engraver and William Luson Thomas, later to found the *Graphic* – were struck by Keene's idiosyncratic lifestyle. Although only in his twenties he was fast becoming a character, a fact that was reinforced by his appearance. Dr Dulcken, who later employed Keene to illustrate his *German Songs*, recorded his impressions at this time: 'I remember him a very grave, saturnine looking young fellow, with a face like a young Don Quixote, shy even to awkwardness with strangers, but lighting up immensely among friends.'[4] Keene probably adopted the attitude of a young fogey very early on and acquired all the tastes of middle age when scarcely out of youth. He was already a great bibliophile, hoarding piles of dusty volumes, poring over forgotten authors and displaying a wide knowledge of ancient lore and antiquity. These hobbies were accompanied by constant sketching and equally constant pipe-smoking or rather the filling and re-filling of tiny clay pipes.

Keene had already perfected the habit of smoking from little 'plague-pipes' declaring that they 'had a sweetness of their own unequalled by any modern manufacture'.[5] At various times, Keene acquired examples found on building sites, in the mud of the Thames and other less than salubrious places. He always lit them with an old-fashioned flint and steel and filled them from an ancient brass tobacco box. These little pipes needed constant filling and he would clear out the remains of the last smoke, saturated with nicotine, and secrete them in an old sardine box. When questioned about this habit he replied, 'O those! – those are "dottles". When I do a drawing I think really so good as to deserve a reward, I smoke a pipeful of "dottles". That's what I keep them for.'[6] According to his biographer Layard, these lethal concoctions were strong enough to have poisoned a bargee!

Quite early in his career, Keene's smoking had lost him all sense of taste and smell, which might account for his strange diet, recorded by all who knew him. His breakfast consisted of porridge, bacon cooked to a cinder, fruit tart and jam, all except the porridge notable for sharp flavours. He ate no luncheon and cooked his own dinner, a stew of beefsteak, onions and potatoes cooked for hours and followed by bread and jam and strong coffee. He did not like conversing during these repasts, preferring the stimulus of a book propped up on a coffee pot. It is not surprising that he loathed formality but he also had a great objection to being greeted in the morning and even to shaking hands! Keene's eccentricities were well known but he was greatly respected because his life was totally dedicated to draughtsmanship and illustration.

His life as a working illustrator must have begun while he was still at Whymper's: at least one book, *The Adventures of Dick Boldhero*, 1842, has a title-page by Keene engraved by J.D. Cooper (1823–1904). Practically all Keene's early work was engraved by James Davies Cooper, so it is likely that he was encouraged by this engraver, or that both artist and engraver were apprentices together at Whymper's. Cooper had set himself up as an independent engraver by 1849 at 10 Ely Place, Holborn, and was to distinguish himself as a close collaborator with the colour printer Richard Clay.[7] This happy partnership continued into the late 1840s when Cooper and Keene worked together for various small publishers, notably Burns, Darton & Clark, and Hatchard.

The most important of these early books was *The Life and Surprising Adventures of Robinson Crusoe* published by James Burns in 1847. This is really the first book in which Keene was given his head as illustrator and a number of the original drawings for the illustrations survive (see Plate 1.1, p. 6). The sketches are flowing and well-conceived – Keene's silvery pencil line gives them greater vivacity than they have on the printed page, but they are nevertheless indistinguishable from similar works by Tenniel and Gilbert. The illustrators of the 1840s were still in the mould of Stothard and his successors and were only slowly to learn the power and scale that the medium was to offer. The same year as the *Crusoe* saw Keene contributing to *Green's Nursery Annual*, a child's book from Darton & Co where his handful of illustrations are rather in the style of John Absolon, another Darton artist.

Keene's rather bohemian existence was expanding to include a few artist friends and some amateur patrons. Notable among the last were Mr and Mrs Thomas

1.1   Preliminary studies for *Robinson Crusoe*, 1847, one of Keene's earliest commissions.
Pencil on sketch-book leaves.   4 × 7in.   10.5 × 18.5cm.
Michael Broadbent Collection

Barrett of Winterslow Place, London, who invited artist friends for the evening and set a subject for them which was copied into an album. Both Keene and Tenniel contributed to this for a number of years, generally chalk drawings, taken from pasages of literature and history. It was a light-hearted pastime and the album came to be called the 'Book of Beauty', a skit on the drawing-room scrapbooks of similar name that were pouring from the publishers at this time. Keene and Tenniel teased out subjects from Shakespeare, Milton, Dryden, Tasso and Percy's *Reliques* and the Signs of the Zodiac, endowing them with their own comical spirit. They must have been influenced by the vogue for comic histories, the most celebrated being G.A. A'Beckett's *Comical History of England*, illustrated by Leech and published in 1847.

In fact, neither of these young artists' contributions were anything like the books they pretended to satirise but joyous iconoclastic creations that in Tenniel's case prefigured his brilliant comic illustrations in *Alice In Wonderland*. In Keene's case they show he was a great comic artist as well as a great draughtsman, not always evident from his later works. The fact that both artists worked in chalks may reflect the freedom they saw in the lithographic caricatures of France – they were spontaneous autograph works, drawn on the stone with a gallic fire and

1.2   Cavalier Scene from 'The English Civil War', *c.* 1846–50.
      Watercolour.   2 x 3½in.   7 x 9cm.
      Michael Broadbent Collection

passion. French lithographs were greatly admired by W.M. Thackeray and men of the *Punch* circle, but never developed in quite the same way on this side of the Channel. Keene's page for the Barrett album 'Plutarch Up to Date' is a complete pastiche of these French works. Keene's other contributions include a spirited rendering from Shakespeare: 'Henry IV eats too many Lampreys', 'Knight and Saracen' (see Plate 1.3, p. 9) and 'Tragedy of the Italians'. A characteristic page is 'Virgo The Virgin' where a contemporary artist is putting finishing touches to a travesty of the Virgin Queen's portrait! (See Plate 1.4, p. 10.) These drawings, now in a private collection, are only a selection of the 37 subjects he was to add to the album. They prove not only his grasp of humorous draughtsmanship and the imaginative, but show him to have been an admirable colourist in the pastel tints of the chalk tradition.

Keene's five years with the Messrs Whymper were the traditional training for an engraver but apart from this he had no training as an artist. Although he was an instinctive draughtsman, he was well aware of his own shortcomings and set about improving his hand and his knowledge of nature in the late 1840s. In about 1848, he began to attend the informal gatherings of artists meeting in Clipstone Street, Fitzroy Square, later to be known as the Langham Artists Society. There, professional artists met on Friday nights to draw from life, the models being nude or costumed on alternate weeks. Keene needed this sort of discipline and was a regular attender for the next fourteen years. He developed greatly as a figure artist, gradually producing astonishing nude studies, superbly modelled and with a marvellous understanding of light and shadow. He also began to experiment in watercolour at this time, a medium that he did not use often but worked in very successfully.

Among the early watercolours are scenes from the English Civil War, always a subject dear to the heart of the artist (see Plate 1.2, p. 7). One in a private collection shows a helmeted figure rushing through a darkened interior, the use of colour wash very assured and free. Some later Langham life studies also exist, very flowing watercolours of male nudes, the shading handled with great dexterity. He continued to do Cavalier subjects at Clipstone Street in the early 1850s. Two are in the Fitzwilliam: 'Preparing for the Fight' in watercolour on grey paper, and 'Fight between Cavalier and Roundhead Horsemen' in chalk and grey wash. A further drawing in pencil with some watercolour is 'Soldiers outside an Inn' which harks back to the eighteenth-century draughtsmen whom Keene admired (see Plate 1.6, p. 13).

Clipstone Street was a convivial atmosphere in which to work and among his friends were Carl Haag, E.J. Poynter and John Tenniel, some of whom did portraits of each other when they were not concentrating on the set subject. When the Artists Society finally moved from Clipstone Street to Langham Chambers in 1856, Keene moved in to occupy the vacated old sheds with his painter friend and

1.3 Knight and Saracen. Drawn for 'The Book of Beauty', c. 1846–50.
Black and coloured chalks. 8 × 6in. 22.5 × 15cm.
Michael Broadbent Collection

9

1.4   Virgo The Virgin. Drawn for 'The Book of Beauty', *c.* 1846–50.
Black and coloured chalks.   8³/₄ × 5³/₄in.
Michael Broadbent Collection

amateur photographer J.D. Wingfield, an arrangement that lasted till 1863.

The six years that elapsed between Keene's leaving Whymper's and his first appearance in *Punch* must have been testing times for the young artist. His occasional work as an illustrator would have been supplemented by hack-work for the engravers and perhaps help from the widowed Mrs Keene. The repetitive hours at the wood-engraving bench at Whymper's had made Keene a craftsman if not a great artist; he had learnt a system and an attitude of mind that was to stand him in good stead. In 1853, Keene had an opportunity to work for the new illustrated press which was beginning to create a new breed of artist reporters. His old Ipswich friend Samuel Read had become manager of the art department of the *Illustrated London News* which had been founded by the Ingram family a decade earlier. Read was sent to the Crimea to record the war and Keene was employed to work up his friend's drawings from rough sketches. 'By degrees Keene dropped into a regular course of journalistic illustration,' Layard records,

> and was required to dance attendance – a class of work always distasteful to him – at political meetings, ministerial receptions, soirees, and such like to make sketches of the rooms and company. As time went on, and he found himself able to do without pot-boiling work of that kind, he gave it up, and confined himself to drawing subjects for the Christmas numbers and any special occasions.[8]

Some of his Crimean subjects are still extant and show him to have been a very able military artist. (He was always fascinated by soldiering and later joined the Volunteer regiment.) 'A Military Encounter' of 1854–55 probably depicts Sebastopol and demonstrates his ability to handle crowded scenes as well as the single figures for which he became well known. Slightly later in 1855, he was employed by Messrs Dickinson of Bond Street, to make large drawings of Sebastopol based on eye witness accounts from the trenches (see Plate 1.7, p. 15). It is possible that some of these subjects relate to that second commission.[9] His last contribution to the *Illustrated London News* was at Christmas 1858. None of this experience was wasted, years later a theatrical crowd was needed in a drawing (Plate 3.13, p. 63) and was done by him with consummate mastery; equally, distant figures and buildings could be rendered with great skill.

Despite his bohemianism and greater ease in the society of other artists, Keene was still very much a homing pigeon. He never lived at his places of work, usually lodging within reach of his studio but returning again and again to his family circle. Like many other eminent Victorians from large families, Keene had no need to abandon bachelorhood when he had the comfortable fireside of his mother, brother and unmarried sisters to resort to. Mrs Mary Sparrow Keene, who had pressed so hard to get Keene established, was still a benevolent matriarch, loving to have her young and not-so-young descendants around her. Alfred Corbould, the artist and Keene's schoolfellow, had married Mary, Keene's eldest sister in 1848. Alfred Corbould, who was studying with Benjamin Robert Herring became

1.5 Lady resting in a studio, *c.* 1850–55.
Pen and ink.   160 x 192in.   406.5 x 487.5cm.
Visitors of the Ashmolean Museum.

Scolar Press
Marketing Services Manager
Gower House
Croft Road
Aldershot
Hampshire
GU11 3BR

Books on Music from Scolar Press

Scolar Press is a leading publisher in music studies with a high reputation for scholarship and excellence. Our publishing list continues to expand to complement our existing titles in the areas of Medieval, Renaissance and Baroque Music, Vocal and Choral Music, 19th and 20th Century Music and British Music and Musicians.

We would be pleased to send you details of our publications in the areas that interest you. Just fill in the section below and we will send you the relevant information.

Please send me information on the books you publish in the following subject areas and details of special sales or offers:

Name _____

Job title and Institution (if relevant) _____

Address _____

_____ Postcode _____

If you know anyone else who would appreciate this service please give their details here:

_____

X2067

☐ If you do not wish to receive information from other organizations please tick here

1.6　Soldiers outside an inn, *c.* 1855–60.
Watercolour over pencil.　　6³⁄₄ × 9¹⁄₂in.　　17 × 24cm.
Michael Cook Collection.

a member of this close family circle and was often in Keene's company. This still left Ann Sparrow Keene and Kate Lever Keene at home and for the time being their younger brother Henry Eddowes Keene, who was also an amateur artist. Old Mrs Keene had been living at Lewisham from 1844 and so Keene himself had to have a separate establishment near his work. The young artist spent his hours of relaxation in their company, where pets and songbirds abounded and the intrusion of outsiders was not needed.

Mrs Keene moved to a house, the White Cottage, on the edge of Hammersmith in about 1853–54 and this became the focus for much of Keene's drawing in the next few years. In this slightly claustrophobic atmosphere Keene's introspective nature seems to have been accentuated. Here he used his mother and sisters as models (where else would he have observed a young lady lying on a bed?) and absorbed his immediate surroundings with visual effect, each object observed with a detailed almost manic intensity. This period was among Keene's happiest, before the loss of his much-loved mother and one sister, and before the old house itself was pulled down. Much later du Maurier records a visit to the White Cottage in October 1863, set down with delightful candour:

> I afterwards slept at Keene's in Hammersmith, and breakfasted with his mother and sisters next morning. It's a funny old tumbledown sort of house, just what one would fancy Keene living in; two nice gardens utterly uncultivated and overrun with weeds; one of his sisters rather nice looking – very plain and unsophisticated sort of people. What a splendid fellow Keene is. I like him more and more every day.[10]

These years at the White Cottage, from 1853 to 1868, are the most productive of Keene's life. The tranquil setting and the great love he had for the inhabitants was probably more conducive to advance in his art than at any other time. In those two decades he achieved a mastery of draughtsmanship undreamed of in the 1840s and an assurance of manner that was rare in Victorian art. That period saw him established at *Punch* magazine and prolific in other publications; it saw him recognised for the first time by his fellow artists and deeply influenced by the Pre-Raphaelites, it saw him in contact with European trends in the arts. These aspects will be dealt with specifically in following chapters. What is important to appreciate is that, by 1853, the Charles Keene who was admired and respected by his contemporaries was beginning to emerge from anonymity.

Notes

1. Layard, 1892, p. 7.
2. ibid., p. 7.
3. ibid., p. 19.
4. ibid., p. 25.
5. ibid., p. 28.

1.7   Sebastopol Siege, *c.* 1855.
Pen, ink and wash.   8¹/₄ × 6in.   22.3 × 15.4cm.
Michael Cook Collection.

6. ibid., p. 31.
7. Engen, 1985.
8. Layard, 1892, p. 34.
9. ibid., p. 39.
10. Du Maurier, 1951, p. 174.

2 Pre-Raphaelite draughtsman

Few of the early commentators on Keene make any reference to the influence upon him of the great art movement of his time – Pre-Raphaelitism. It is often forgotten that the Pre-Raphaelites were not simply painters but illustrators; the original organ of their movement, *The Germ*, contained illustrations and scarcely one among the first or second generation of Pre-Raphaelites failed to contribute to a book. Although Keene was unknown to their charmed circle in 1847, he was of their age group and the passion and intensity of their draughtsmanship was soon to spill over into the art schools, drawing societies and studios of their contemporaries.

George du Maurier, a very perceptive colleague, noticed a change in Keene's work between 1855 and 1864 and notes it in a letter to his friend Tom Armstrong:

> Your notion of going to an academy at night is excellent; just the very thing you want, though we shall be deuced sorry not to have you smoking the cigarette of peace in our hospitable mansion. But I think you ought to draw draw draw till all is blue, for you can paint as well as anybody. Old Keene has reached his great perfection through this: for years I believe he has spent his two hours at the Langham, and his early drawings which I have been looking at in old Punches have just the faults of your paintings; a certain ungainliness which came from his difficulty in imitating nature engrossing all his attention, & not letting him think of anything else. Now he draws so easily that he can do it by feeling in the same way that a good sportsman will shoot a snipe, more by the feeling of his gun with relation to his hands & shoulder than by taking aim with his eye. Old Keene is more than 10 years older than you, and the drawings I refer to were done six or seven years ago.[1]

Du Maurier, writing in 1864, is a little unconvincing on dates. Keene's mature style was fully developed by 1855 and there was only a little *Punch* work before that time. Pennell records that change:

> In his very early work for the wood-engraver you can see that Keene was influenced more or less by Leech, whose drawings could be engraved, I imagine, fairly well … Keene's style of drawing for publication became bolder and bolder as time went on. For his own pleasure he continued to make with his pen little masterpieces which, in their refinement, are worthy to rank with the etchings of Rembrandt and Whistler.[2]

Layard *does* refer to a watercolour of Keene's Strand studio which is rendered in Pre-Raphaelite detail. He adds, 'There is no doubt that Keene was at one time

2.1 Self-Portrait with Fellow Artist, c. 1860.
Pen and ink. 4 × 5¾in. 10 × 14.5cm.
Michael Broadbent Collection.

2.2 A River Bed, 1860s. 5 × 8¼in. 12.5 × 21cm.
Pen and brown ink.
The Visitors of The Ashmolean Museum.

much influenced by the movement of Holman Hunt and his associates.'[3] If this study comes from about 1855 (he left the Strand in 1857) it could date from the years when his drawing took on a new maturity and a greater virtuosity, akin to the drawings of Millais and Hunt. This passionate vision must have been in the air, firing the young draughtsman of the 1850s, but it is also likely that personal contact deepened his commitment to nature and drawing from the life. Early in 1854, Keene made the acquaintance of the minor Pre-Raphaelite painter and collector George Price Boyce (1826–1897). This casual meeting grew into an intimate friendship in the 1860s, Boyce being a devotee of Bewick engravings, singing and antiquarianism generally. Through Boyce he must have got to know D.G. Rossetti and J.E. Millais, both of whom were the subject of ink portraits. But he did not know them well as is shown by the rather formal letters to Millais written at the end of his life.

Boyce must have been the stimulus, the two artists playing chess together (Keene was known to take a half-hour to make a move) and sharing models. Of the artistic cliques of the 1850s, Keene was definitely in the Langham one, although he does refer to 'the Rossetti set' in his letters. The studies of Keene's studio in Clipstone Street all date from this period and Layard rightly refers to the 'Pre-Raphaelite character of this drawing' (Layard, p. 24).[4] His very fine ink study now in the British Museum reflects this same idiom and must have been done around this period. This lovely sketch, inscribed 'A foggy day. Painter cleaning his skylight' (see Plate 2.5, p. 23), must date between 1859 (from the watermark of the paper) and 1863 when he vacated the premises. It was actually used in *Punch* on 14 February 1863 over the title 'A Black Fog'. With hatching of incredible delicacy and subtlety, Keene depicts the sharp contrasts of light and shade in his cavernous studio. The artist himself perches on a box placed on a table as he attempts to scrape the skylight. In the foreground, his model, caught in mid-pose, lolls impatiently in her seat waiting for the sketching to begin again. The woman, taken off the streets, could have been any of the girls used by Boyce or indeed by Rossetti or Whistler. The minute observation of light on the most remote surfaces of the interior, on the silk of the model's dress and on the heavier textures of hanging coats, links Keene with this powerful and obsessive concern for reality, typical of the Pre-Raphaelite drawings of modern life.

It was at precisely this time (1860) that Keene developed a friendship with the painter Henry Stacy Marks. Marks mentions that he was 'much influenced by the Pre-Raphaelite School at this time' and his sketches bear it out.[5] Keene and Marks met at the Langham where so many of Keene's friendships began and Marks perceptively recalls how important the non-commercial part of his drawing life was to Keene. 'Many of these drawings,' Marks wrote, 'revealed the more romantic and imaginative side of Keene's nature of which those who knew him only by his works for *Punch* have little or no idea.'[6]

2.3   Trees in a Park, 1860s.
Pen and ink.   15.4 x 20.2cm.
Victoria and Albert Museum.

2.4   Birdcage in the garden door of the White Cottage, 1862.
Pen and ink. $6^{3}/_{4} \times 4^{1}/_{4}$in.   17 × 11cm.
Michael Broadbent Collection.

2.5   Artist Cleaning His Skylight. Self-portrait of Keene and model in the Langham studio,
c. 1862.
Pen and ink.   10 × 8in.
Trustees of the British Museum.

Keene's extraordinary knowledge of Londoners and Thameside characters meant that he had struck up acquaintance with the Greenwich watermen. These folk ran up the estuary from Kent to supply Billingsgate Market with fish, using hatch-boats, so-called because a long hatch ran down the centre. The two artists chartered a hatch-boat, the *William and Mary*, in August 1860 to cruise down to the mouth of the Thames. They called in at Queenborough, Gillingham and Benfleet, sampling the fare in the various taverns and capturing a bit of the local atmosphere. Marks adds:

> Keene was accustomed at that time to draw straight from any object in pen and ink, without preparatory pencilling, as a means of obtaining certainty and sureness of hand. Wishing to emulate his example, I began to do likewise. Each of us wore an ink bottle suspended from our waistcoat-buttons ... We drew each other, the boatmen, parts of the vessel, occasionally going ashore for a bit of landscape.[7]

These harbourscapes and landscapes, so rare in Keene's *oeuvre*, show him to be a brilliant portrayer of the natural world, buildings, tree shapes, jetties and shingle, even if they are not populated by his well-known figures. Such studies were undoubtedly used in his commercial work, but the motivation here is sheer pleasure, and enjoyment is evident in every stroke of the pen. Keene could render the grain on a piece of wood or the foliage of a particular hedgerow with all the precision of his Pre-Raphaelite friends; the spirit of the movement pervaded a whole generation, even those who would not necessarily have espoused the cause. Among the finest landscapes in this group is a scene in a park (see Plate 2.3, p. 21), where the gnarled boles of oak trees are finely executed in their summer dress, every slight reflection of light on the twisted bark lovingly interpreted. The same undeviating line can be found in drawings of dry riverbeds (see Plate 2.2, p. 19), pigeon houses, boulders, and even on the metal and wood fixtures of a channel boat.

Pennell echoes Stacy Marks in saying that Keene's work was sharply divided between those drawings made for pleasure and those for publication:

> It was no surprise to me to find a large number of landscapes among Keene's unpublished drawings. One has only to look at the moors and meadows and hills that stretch away beyond his gillies and rustics and sportsmen to be sure they were never faked. But I was amazed at the beauty and perfection of execution he put into these sketches.[8]

But in his magnificent volume on Keene's drawings, Joseph Pennell evinces astonishment that Keene should have had any connection with the Pre-Raphaelite artists. However, he goes on to say that two or three drawings 'look as if they had been inspired by Millais' *Isabella* at Liverpool'.[9] Pennell picks up the point that some of these artists certainly admired Keene but might have distanced themselves from a man associated with *Punch*. 'No doubt,' Pennell continues,

> I should be assured that the Pre-Raphaelites never as much as knew of Charles Keene's connection with *Punch*, and much honour would be attributed to them for their ignorance. But

whatever critics may think, Keene was so true an artist that he could afford to admit there were artists beside himself in the world, and he was not too stupid, too pigheaded, too insular, to study them, to admire them, to imitate them.[10]

There is ample evidence for this connection in the drawings themselves, but Pennell was not in possession of as many facts as we are. Du Maurier in particular notes Keene's enthusiasm for these men. He and Keene attended the sale of the Plinth Collection at Christie's in March 1862: '… one of the jolliest and most interesting exhibitions that ever was; I went there with old Keene, who humbled himself before almost every picture in the Room.'[11]

Keene's work was appearing beside that of some of these leading men from 1858 when he contributed to the volumes of the Junior Etching Club. The first publication was *Passages From The Poems of Thomas Hood*, in which Millais illustrated 'The Bridge of Sighs' and 'Ruth' and Keene 'The Lee Shore'. In a later volume from the Club, *Passages From The Modern English Poets*, Keene contributed 'Scene of the Plague in London' and appears alongside work by Millais, Lawless, Marks and others.

Pennell states in his authoritative work how Keene's interest was 'above all for the romance of the every-day life and people about him, the Pre-Raphaelites seeking romance in literature or the past'.[12] This is not strictly true. Keene was passionately interested in historical dramas and costume subjects, 'Scene of the Plague' being only one example, and the Pre-Raphaelite group were fascinated by modern life subjects in much the same way as Keene. The essential social comment on life and what Baudelaire called the 'heroism of modern life' are to be seen as much in the studies and scenes by Keene as they are in Ford Madox Brown's 'Work' or Rossetti's 'Found'. This facet of Pre-Raphaelitism comes closest to Keene in the serious subjects that he undertook in the early 1860s.

In much the same way that the Pre-Raphaelites had been an introspective and tightly-knit group, the Keene family provided a private and closed circle for Charles. The results were a similar intensity of observation and an almost tangible emotion in depicting everyday objects. The fireside and the environs of the White Cottage became places where Keene worked out not only his responses to light and shade but even more the love and tenderness towards his family which he was unable to put into words. This is nowhere more evident than in his superb ink drawing 'Birdcage in the Garden Door of the White Cottage' of 1865–69 (see Plate 2.4, p. 22). This is no *Punch* study but the evocation of peace and tranquility that Keene so much valued in the persons of his mother and sisters. The family's love of pets, their unspoken understanding of each other, their devotion to the simple life, all are manifest in this drawing. The light catches the old tree trunk; beyond is the untamed garden that du Maurier noticed on his visit. The treatment of the wooden door and especially the build-up of lines to indicate the folds of the curtain are as good as any Millais or Rossetti. Layard refers to this as the 'Front

2.6   Two Artists working by lamplight in a studio, *c.* 1860–62.
       Pen and brown ink on grey paper.   7 x 5in.   19 x 12.5cm
       The Tate Gallery.

2.7   Portrait of William Morris, *c.* 1869.
       Black chalk with heightening.   3³/₄ x 4in.   9.5 x 11cm.
       The Visitors of The Ashmolean Museum.

Door' but it must be the garden door.

Another significant drawing, rather different in character is the portrait of his mother which dates from the same years (see Plate 3.2, p. 47). She is shown as a benevolent matriarch, sitting contentedly in her chair with a great spread of bombazine skirt before her. By her side is her table and work-basket and she appears to have just opened a letter. This sketch was used in *Punch* twice – 23 November 1867 and 17 February 1872 – demonstrating how often he returned to his family for inspiration as models.

The most important opinion about Keene's work at this time would be from the pen of a Pre-Raphaelite painter. No such commentary has come to light. The nearest approach to this however is a remarkable essay by 'Drypoint' on 'The Art of Punch' which was published in the *Spectator* on 14 and 21 September 1861. The author was William Michael Rossetti (1829–1919), brother of D.G. Rossetti and the nearest we can get to the authentic opinion of that influential group. The passages on Charles Keene are so remarkable that it seems important to reprint the whole section, which has not been noticed for 130 years.

'Mr Charles Keene has not been connected with *Punch* for more than seven or eight years,' Rossetti writes, 'but in that time he has made visible progress. Many of his earlier drawings are black and heavy through over-elaboration; those of today, while equally careful, are brilliant, free, and life-like. The two chief characteristics of his style are individuality and conscientiousness. His heads all look like portraits, the minutest details of character are never omitted, and every part of his drawing has nature for its basis. Mr Keene delights in setting himself tasks of artistic difficulty requiring much time and patience in their accomplishment. Whatever he does, he determines shall be done thoroughly. Thus, to take a common instance, in drawing a cab or cart wheel (a foreshortened one pleases him best), Mr Keene will take care that it shall be as exactly like a wheel as he can make it, that it shall be so true in its formation that no coach-maker shall be able to find fault with it. It may not be a matter of vital importance, perhaps, to draw wheels in this careful manner in an ordinary woodcut, and Mr Leech, whose wheels are not even round, shows that they may be drawn with the greatest recklessness. But the pleasure is the same in amount, though of a different kind, that an artist feels in looking at Mr Leech's dashing resemblances to a wheel and Mr Keene's actual portraiture of one.

'This incident of the wheel may appear trivial to some readers, but it is not really so. In the first place, a wheel is by no means an easy object to draw truly, and then, if we find an artist so faithful in his inanimate objects, we may generally rely upon his truthfulness in higher things, such as the features and expressions of men and women. Accordingly, when Mr Keene introduces us to Buffles, of the Blankshire Volunteers, he gives not only the proper number of buttons to his coat, and a faithful delineation of all his equipments, but he stamps the character of the face and figure of Buffles with such force that the truth of the portrait is at once recognisable. Mr Keene's love of outdoor nature is as strongly pronounced as Mr Leech's. His landscape backgrounds are charmingly real. He has not the extensive knowledge of the world that Mr Leech possesses, nor is his range of character so varied. He chiefly reproduces the dining-room waiter, the cab or omnibus driver, and the rifle volunteer. Sometimes he portrays the "swell", but his chief pet is the artist.

'Mr Keene has depicted him under a variety of aspects – taking in the milk for his tea, writhing under the remarks of lay critics, getting enthusiastic over Macaulay's *Ivry*, talking "shop" in a railway carriage, and shocking an old lady by the indifference with which he talks of knocking off little girls' heads or moving his "properties", and having a dispute with the cabman about the lay figure which cabby wants to charge for as a "hextra person, 'cos I see she wos a hinwalid". I hear of much complaint against Mr Keene amongst the more "select" artists, for what they consider such "libels on the profession". With such very thin-skinned gentlemen it would be idle to remonstrate, but a more tangible objection to Mr Keene's artist drawings is that he only presents us with one type of the class – a being who can afford to be well, though sometimes eccentrically, clad, but who prefers to paint, seated on a penitential trestle in a studio, picturesque, perhaps, but scarcely comfortable – a sort of carpenter's cast-off shed, which admits the wind through many a chink, and the temperature of which is scarcely rendered endurable by a stove with a perpetually smoking chimney. Mr Keene might now and then favour us with the "lavender-kid artist", whose clothes make so capital an advertisement for his tailor, and who has a painting-room in the neighbourhood of Regent Street or Piccadilly; the "man of the day", whose talk is of dukes and countesses, or the drawling Pre-Raphaelite, who finds everything painted by his clique "awfully jolly", and everything else "awful rot"; or the artist who attributes his want of success to ill-luck instead of to his bad painting, and considers that the Royal Academicians, unanimous for once in their lives, have leagued themselves into a conspiracy to crush him. These and others must be more familiar to Mr Keene than to the present writer, and I hope that in his next artist cut we may behold the results of his experience.

'Political caricature is never attempted by Mr Keene. He confines himself to conversational subjects, initial letters, and headings to the prefaces and indexes. His jokes are laboured and not always obvious. Judging from other illustrations by Mr Keene, such as the admirable series of the "Good Fight" in *Once A Week*, I should say his genius is rather grave than gay. But as no man can be constantly aiming at a target without frequently "making a bulls-eye", so Mr Keene cannot fail of being humorous sometimes. As an early example of intensified fun, I should mention "Mr Popplewit", an inexperienced sportsman, who, having returned home from a day's shooting, allows the gun to go off in the hall while in a perpendicular position. The charge passes through three floors, blowing up the pet spaniel, and shivering the chandelier to atoms in the first – smashing a looking-glass in the second – scattering the childrens' toys in the nursery on the third floor, and finally, scaring the cats on the roof of the house. There is much grotesque drollery in the group of Gorillas which heads the preface to the last volume, and others might be mentioned did space permit.

'Mr Keene's present style is large, broad, and energetic. He draws with firmness and power. He improves gradually, but surely, though sometimes his progress is marked by leaps. One of these leaps took place two weeks ago, in a drawing of two artists sketching on stilts, which, regarded from an artistic point of view, is, perhaps, the best. Mr Keene has achieved Sea, beach, boats, and figures, drawn with a light but certain hand, while the brilliant sunny effect deserves the highest praise. I have never seen a picture bearing Mr Keene's name, and hear that he does not paint. It is a great pity, for he is evidently the owner of high pictorial powers. The demands on his time are doubtless great, but he surely does not lack the inclination to paint, and if he has the inclination, can he not continue to shape the opportunity? It is out of no disrespect to Mr Keene's *Punch* drawings, but because I think so highly of them, that I believe him to be capable of finer and more durable art, and, in common with many others, I should be glad to find the name of Charles Keene in the Royal Academy Catalogue for 1862.'[13]

Rossetti's understanding of Keene's great draughtsmanship is more fulsome than that of most of his colleagues on *Punch*. The very criticism that Rossetti levels against him for his drab treatment of the artist's studio is actually a compliment; Keene was depicting his own workplace with Pre-Raphaelite accuracy! Nor was Rossetti to know that Keene was experimenting with oil colour at exactly this moment.

2.8   Study of a man and girl on a horse for *Once a Week* 1860.
Pencil.   3 x 6¼in.   10 x 16cm.
Michael Broadbent Collection.

A further link is provided by the proof that both Keene and the Pre-Raphaelites were studying the same sources. Dr Dulcken mentions that in 1855 or 1856, Keene developed a great interest in a published work of the German artist Adolph Menzel (1815–1905). Menzel had been working on a huge book *Uniforms in the Army of Frederick the Great* from about 1840 and it was published in English in 1844. The plates were issued in parts in 1853 and 1856 and it is probably these that Keene had obtained. Menzel's meticulous draughtsmanship would have appealed to Keene, the all-absorbing quest for detail and his quoted remark that he was drawing as if he would never see the object again. Most of all Keene would have appreciated the true professionalism in Menzel's work, individually conceived for the art of wood-engraving. At exactly this time the Pre-Raphaelites were fired with admiration for Menzel and were copying his early works.[14]

Was the brilliance of Keene's draughtsmanship undervalued by his contemporaries? Both Forrest Reid and Joseph Pennell remark on the lack of serious literature illustrated by Keene in the 1860s, a time when even minor men had ample employment. This rather echoes Rossetti's sapient remark that his inclination was more 'grave than gay'. Of his opportunities to illustrate great classics, one was turned down by Keene himself – the Dalziels' suggestion of illustrating *Don Quixote* – and the other was never reprinted in book form. Reid concluded 'that it seems only too probable that Charles Keene as an illustrator was not in great demand'. The *Don Quixote* would have been a superb chance for Keene to employ his great knowledge of costume, but the undertaking, eventually brought out with Boyd Houghton's engravings, would have been too big a project for Keene with his dislike of commercial pressures and deadlines.

The two novels by George Meredith, *Evan Harrington* and *Verner's Pride*, are a different case as they were fully illustrated and came out in the periodical *Once a Week* which was a sister magazine to *Punch*. These stories were ideal for Keene's matchless line: they were contemporary tales which the artist was always best at bringing to life and they were wide ranging in figure subjects. Pennell commented, 'His drawings . . . are as modern as Mr Meredith's novel.'[16] Pennell in fact saw in these designs of 1860 a change of direction from the constraints of the wood-engraved style and the *Punch* conventions of Leech:

> I think he must first have broken loose, have refused the restrictions they would have imposed on him, in his illustrations for *Evan Harrington*, so obviously is he here trying to express himself in his own fashion, so unmistakeably has the refinement and delicacy characteristic of his unpublished drawings survived, though too often his exquisite modelling of a face has been translated into the simplest lines or cut out altogether.[17]

This is simply another recognition of that purifying of style between 1855 and 1860, already noticed by George du Maurier.

In the case of *Evan Harrington*, George Meredith records that there was no consultation between artist and author and that although Keene had been free to

2.9   Study of a girl, 1860s.
Pencil and ink.   7 x 4¹/₂in.   20 x 11.5cm.
Michael Broadbent Collection.

chose his own subjects 'the pictures gave the novelist entire satisfaction'.[18] Keene is absolute master of this story of modern life and excels particularly in its more rustic aspects. He begins in April 1860 with head pieces that have a touch of the burlesque but none of the carelessness of that great illustrator Leech. But they gradually develop a certain classical beauty by 17 March 1860: even a couple caught in converse compare most favourably with a Millais sylph on the opposite page. From here onwards the groups at the beginning of each chapter are superb, the family at the fair on 7 April, a couple in a conservatory on 28 April and the horse ride on 12 May (see Plate 2.8, p. 29). Both female and male dress are beautifully observed and Keene employs that favourite trick of his, capturing people from the back viewpoint, thereby wooing the reader into the greater intimacy of the situation.

His women are enchanting, dispelling the notion that he cannot depict elegance or society, one of the finest being that of a girl peering round a tree trunk of 28 July 1860, and as competent as any by Millais. These fine things continue more or less until the story's conclusion on 13 October 1860. After a short gap with one 'medieval' engraving, Keene was back to illustrating a contemporary novelette *Sam Bentley's Christmas* in December (see Plate 2.10, p. 33). Why he was not given the lion's share of novels it is difficult to understand, particularly as Tenniel's drawings of contemporary society are so feeble. Keene re-emerged in the autumn of 1861 with some lovely designs for *Lilian's Perplexities* but by the end of that year Fred Walker was doing the rural subjects and du Maurier had won his spurs for society pictures.

Keene's next opportunity was for large head pieces to Mrs Henry Wood's *Verner's Pride*, serialised in the magazine from 28 June 1862. Here once again Keene's strengths are in the country scenes and the modelling of his figures. Not much appears to be lost in the engraving but how exquisite the original pen drawings must have been. The illustrations for Chapters 9 and 17 are as glorious as anything produced by the later Idyllic school of the 1860s! Unfortunately Keene's talents were not employed for every instalment of this lengthy romance, so that may have had something to do with the pictures not being reprinted in book form, but their power is sustained right to the end.

George Meredith and Mrs Henry Wood were the only major Victorian authors that Keene was asked to illustrate independently of *Punch*. Not quite all, for he was also asked to draw a frontispiece and initial letter for George Eliot's 'Brother Jacob' in the *Cornhill Magazine* for 1864. This was, rather surprisingly, his only representation in the prestigious *Cornhill*. Layard wrote of this unique partnership, 'It would be hard to conceive of a more satisfactory wedding of pen and pencil.'[19] It is easy to believe that a more enlightened editorship or a less coercive *Punch* could have allied Keene to Thackeray, Trollope or Wilkie Collins.

If this *Once a Week* period was a high point in Keene's development, it is a pity

2.10   Study for 'Sam Bentley's Christmas' for *Once a Week* 1860.
Pen and ink.   5¹/₂ × 5in.   14 × 12.5cm.
The Tate Gallery.

2.11   Study of man's head, from the Langham, early 1860s.
Pen and ink.   4¹/₄ × 4¹/₄in.   11 × 10.8cm.
Michael Cook Collection.

that so little survives from it. In the late 1850s and early 1860s the artist was still drawing the finished composition on the block for it to be cut away by the engraver, so that no completed drawings survived. What we have are fragments of this most productive period: a number of superb studies and a few drawings on tracing paper ready to be transferred to the block. It is interesting to note that these sketches and studies were not highly regarded by the Victorians, possibly not by the artist. As Pennell notes, the Fine Art Society exhibition of Keene's drawings in 1891 had only the finished *Punch* work framed; the studies we value today were just in portfolios.[20]

Keene had appeared in *Once a Week* from the very first number on 2 July 1859, allowed to stay because Leech was present to tackle the comedy and Millais to evoke the poetic. It actually makes a very interesting comparison, the brilliant carelessness of Leech's more 'Georgian' humour, the measured beauty of Millais' damsels and the robust characterisations of Keene. He had been given Charles Reade's 'A Good Fight' to illustrate (mentioned by Rossetti), a medieval subject, which presumably Bradbury and Evans trusted him with because of his great knowledge of costume. Keene's mock medieval engravings are done in the Germanic style, rather linear and frieze-like with little contrast and large areas of white. They are meant to echo the woodcuts of Durer, which were extremely popular and idolised by the Pre-Raphaelites and by Keene's friend Stacy Marks. Although there is a slightly melodramatic element to these headpieces (they are mostly at the beginning of each chapter to give continuity), they are superbly conceived, particularly that of 2 September 1859 where a young woman is led through a glade, and 10 September 1859, a superb head of a pony. These mirror the rustic medievalism and the gestural quality of Pre-Raphaelitism to which he was so clearly linked. 'A Good Fight' was the only one of these magazine serials to be re-issued as a book with Keene's illustrations. Charles Reade's novel later appeared as *The Cloister and The Hearth* in 1890.

As we have seen, little du Maurier was determined to get into the magazine. To his mother he writes in May 1860, 'Keene's going out of town and I wish to exploit his absence as I have done that of Leech and Millais; such is everybody's advice.'[21] Despite du Maurier's blatant opportunism, Keene befriended him and was one of the people to propose him for *Punch* after Leech's death. Keene was never political like du Maurier and was easily outgunned by the younger man's manoeuvres. This may account for the fact that Keene gradually faded out of *Once a Week* by 1867.

Apart from these classic novels, the most important book undertaken by Keene was probably *Mrs Caudle's Curtain Lectures* by Douglas Jerrold, the perennial tale of matrimonial harassment which had become a firm favourite with the first generation of *Punch* readers. Popularised through the illustrations of Leech, some of which had become enduring images of the 1840s, it would have been impossible for any other artist to tackle these subjects before Leech's death in 1864. Bradbury and Evans were fairly quick off the mark in commissioning Keene in 1865 to make 60 new drawings, presumably for the Christmas market of that year, although the title page is dated 1866.

By a brilliant stroke the publishers let Keene illustrate the text as gentle comedy rather than as burlesque as had been the case with Leech. Layard noticed this necessary change to suit the more sophisticated market of the 1860s: 'There is in them a catching of Nature at her most humorous moments, without a particle of exaggeration, which is, when understood, perfectly astonishing.'[22]

The volume begins with a notable colour frontispiece, unusual in Keene's *oeuvre*, depicting the hapless Mr Caudle returning late to see the shadow of the formidable Mrs Caudle reflected on the blind. This coloured frontispiece is probably by the colour printers Day & Sons. The embossed and gold-stamped cover by Edmond & Remnants shows a four-post bedstead with candle. The book is printed on green paper and superbly designed throughout, a great compliment to Keene's magnificent series of illustrations.

Keene's strong decorative sense is shown in the 37 initial letters which are conceived with immense wit and originality. Measuring only about four inches square, they pack in the detail of the story admirably: a young woman on a rainy city street, a maid-servant at the range, a laundress hanging out washing, a beach scene, a game of billiards and a stroll on the pier. All are handled with consummate artistry and detail in these tiny spaces. They are only the prelude to

2.12   Portrait of Mrs H.E. Keene, early 1860s.
        Pen and ink.   2 x 3in.   5 x 7.5cm.
        Michael Cook Collection.

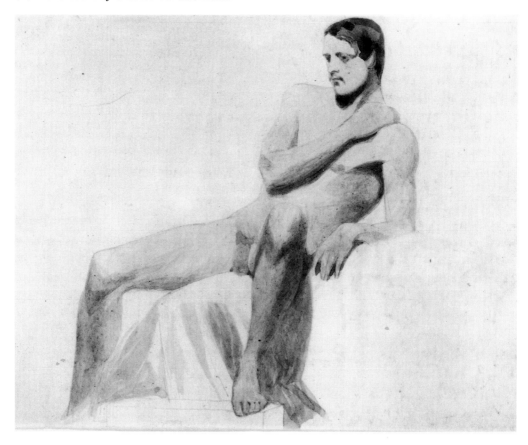

2.13   Male seated nude, Langham study, early 1860s.
Pencil and watercolour.   4 x 6¼in.   10 x 16cm.
Michael Broadbent Collection.

the half-page illustrations. There is tremendous characterisation but no caricature
(Keene was no caricaturist) so Caudle and his friend on page 3 and Caudle with
his wife's dress on page 10 have a naturalness and charm all of their own. Keene
was no stranger to difficult compositions and we find Caudle in his nightshirt –
one of the famous back views, Caudle at the Greenwich Fair – a crowded scene,
and Caudle at a convivial male evening – dramatic use of light and shade. The
artist was an intense assimilator of the world around him, as minute an observer
as Dickens, Thackeray or Trollope in print, or Madox Brown and Holman Hunt
in paint. He saw among his middle-class friends masses of hen-pecked Caudles,
dominating Mrs Caudles and bubbling maid-servants. But it is a mystery how
Keene the bohemian bachelor was able to capture with such truth, ladies in
milliners' shops and the more intimate sides of a Victorian marriage when he knew
so little about them! Apart from the matronly Mrs Caudle he has created some

lovely young girls in small round hats; the sisterly kiss on page 125 is masterly. Even if the tale ends with a touch of pathos, Keene is able to treat the widowed Caudle in a lightsome manner.

A charming excursion by Keene into the demi-monde is provided by *The Cambridge Grisette* by Herbert Vaughan, 1862, for which he made 17 illustrations. Vaughan was a Bradbury and Evans author, a contributor to *Once a Week*, and an ideal partner for Keene in this slightly seedy romance of the young. The studies for the young woman (which exist appropriately enough at Cambridge) are yet another proof that Keene could portray captivating female forms (see Plate 2.16, p. 39). This sketch is exactly the sort of study produced by the Pre-Raphaelites at this time, a stark almost sculptural quality to the lines of the cloak and the modelling confined to the inner folds of the skirt and the head. A closer comparison could be made with James McNeill Whistler's work at the time and his dry point of Annie Hayden. The girl's face seems vaguely familiar, perhaps a Rossetti or Whistler model. She appears again in a more intimate sketch, seated at a table with her hands clasped together, again the bonnet being the most developed part of the ink drawing (see Plate 2.17, p. 40). This is a study for 'The Waiting Room', the most sombre of Keene's illustrations for the book, where the Grisette is watched unobserved by her admirer from the doorway of the darkened room. In many ways it is the closest that Keene comes to the Millais illustrations to Trollope.

Having seen these original sketches, the book itself comes as something of a disappointment. A publisher's blue cloth cover opens up to reveal rather poor wood engravings interpreted by Swain. The Grisette herself has lost much of the coy charm that she has in the original drawing, appearing smug and even frumpish. The initial letters are not quite as witty as in *Caudle* but some of the full-page illustrations have the potential of matching up to that superb work. In particular one would single out 'Chocolate and Madeira' – an interior with a splendid seated figure, 'The Waiting Room' – already mentioned and 'The Boudoir Bar'. Quite exceptional are 'The Langham Rooms' and 'A Billiard Room in the Quadrant' which have great life and expression and are close to the French illustrations of Gavarni. One has only the two drawings to go on, but one must imagine that the sketches for these figures were equally as good and deplore the fact that Keene was so badly served by his engravers.

These crucial years of the early 1860s also formed a period of experiment. He was beginning to take up etching again (dealt with later) and was making trials in tempera with his friend Edwin Edwards. In August 1864 he tells Edwards that he is 'at sea' with his distemper painting and adds 'I don't mind having a dabble with you.'[23] More importantly his few surviving oil paintings seem to date from this time, particularly the two oil self-portraits. The earlier one, perhaps dating from 1860, shows the spare figure of the artist standing by his easel and (because of the

2.14   Irish hawker, *c.* 1865.
       Pen and ink.   4 × 6¼in.   10 × 15.7cm.
       Michael Cook Collection.

2.15   Studies of youths, *Punch*, 8 February 1862.
       Pen and ink.   5½ × 4½in.   14 × 11.3cm.
       Michael Cook Collection.

2.16   Study for the Cambridge Grisette, 1862.
Pen and ink.   7 x 5¹/₄in.   20 x 13.5cm
The Syndics of The Fitzwilliam Museum.

2.17   Study for the Cambridge Grisette seated, 1862.
Pen and ink.   4 × 6in.   10 × 15cm.
Michael Broadbent Collection.

mirror image) painting with his left hand. Keene gazes intently at the viewer and behind him a fiddle hangs on the wall and a Queen Anne chair stands in the background. The second and perhaps more accomplished image, which is now in the Tate Gallery shows the artist seated at his easel on the Queen Anne chair, a red cap jauntily on his head and the right hand, correctly, engaged on the painting. This portrait belonged to two of Keene's closest friends, the artist J.M. Stewart and the collector J.P. Heseltine. Self-portraiture often reveals itself at a time of self-discovery and these two oil paintings emphasise the importance to Keene of these two or three London years.

Another important opportunity came in 1879 when Keene was asked to illustrate Thackeray's *Roundabout Papers*, though the author had been dead for 16 years so that it was hardly a partnership. This was for Smith Elder's Edition de Luxe, the eight drawings appearing in Volume 22 of the 26-volume set, but it is not clear why Keene was chosen. Keene sent the originals to Edward Fitzgerald for his approval. Fitzgerald wrote on 7 July 1880:

> As I am not an Artist (though a very great Author) I will say that Four of your Drawings seemed capital to me … I do not suppose, or wish, that you should make over to me all these Drawings,

which I suppose are the originals from which the Wood was cut. I say I do not 'wish' because I am in my 72nd year; and I now give away rather than accept. But I wished for one at least of your hand; for its own sake, and as a remembrance, for what short time is left to me, of one whom I can sincerely say I regard greatly for himself, as also for those Dunwich days in which I first became known to him. 'Voila qui est dit.'[24]

Even later books, tailor-made for our artist, were the two volumes of *Robert; or Notes from the Diary of a City Waiter* (1885 and 1888), for which he made 31 illustrations (see Plate 5.14, p. 99). Again this was a transcription from the pages of *Punch*. Keene is blissfully at home in the lower-middle class atmosphere of chop-houses, Victorian dens and the male preserves of nearly-smart city gents. He is able to capture perfectly the self-satisfied, gossiping amiability of the waiter with as many asides as in a Restoration comedy.

NOTES

1. Du Maurier, 1951, p. 250.
2. Pennell, J., 1897a, p. 826.
3. Layard, 1892, p. 24.
4. ibid., p. 24.
5. Marks, 1894, p. 50.
6. ibid., p. 110.
7. ibid., p. 112.
8. Pennell, 1897a, p. 826.
9. Pennell, 1897b, p. 19.
10. ibid., p. 19.
11. Du Maurier, 1951, p. 121.
12. Pennell, 1897b, p. 19.
13. *Spectator*, 1861, pp. 1035–36.
14. Rothenstein, 1932, p. 14.
15. *Print Collector's Quarterly*, 17, 1930, p. 30.
16. Pennell, 1897b, p. 21.
17. ibid., p. 30.
18. Layard, 1892, p. 64.
19. ibid., p. 64.
20. Pennell, 1897b, pp. 26–27.
21. Du Maurier, 1951, pp. 18–19.
22. Layard, 1892, p. 104.
23. Fitwilliam, Keene 5.
24. Terhune, 1980, p. 342.

2.18   Study for 'A Woman Hater', *Punch*, 26 October 1867.
Pen and ink.   7 × 11in.   19.5 × 15.9cm
The Tate Gallery.

2.19   Study for 'Perspective,' 1868.
        Pen and ink.   8 x 5½in.   21 x 14cm.
        Michael Cook Collection.

2.20   Full length study of man in a wig, *c*. 1865.
        Pen and ink.   7½ x 3½in.
        Chris Beetles, St James's Ltd.

2.21   Study for 'The Settlers', 1866.
Pen, wash and ink.   7 x 4½in.   20 x 11.5cm.
Visitors of The Ashmolean Museum.

3 Charles Keene of *Punch*

Charles Keene's entry into the pages of *Punch* was slow, almost surreptitious. The transition from serious illustration to Britain's leading comic journal was not an easy move for anyone, least of all for a great draughtsman. John Leech, who was a frustrated painter found the magazine that nurtured him an awkward incubus in later life; du Maurier, a frustrated novelist, may have felt the same. Many of the classic illustrators gave the publication a wide berth and such artists as J.E. Millais preferred not to appear under their own names.

In December 1851, Keene made his first drawing for *Punch* at the request of his friend Henry Silver who was already a writer for the magazine. Silver suggested the subject – A Sketch of the New Paris Street-sweeping Machines – referring to the cannon used in the bloody *coup d'état*. Unable to draw for the wood engraver, Silver called on Keene to ghost his ideas for him. This and three subsequent contributions for Silver's articles remained anonymous, but this concealment could not go on when Mark Lemon, the editor, commended Silver for his work! Silver pleaded with Keene to reveal himself in the autumn of 1851, but the artist continued to sign himself only with a mask until the spring of 1854. Only then was he bold enough to acknowledge his identity and sign with a 'CK'. It was however a further six years before he joined the staff.

As we have already noted, these six years were crucial to his development as an artist: he was finding his way as a line draughtsman and exercising his mind by studying nature in the countryside and in the life class. He was continually sending drawings to *Punch* in these years, but significantly he did not take the step to join the *Punch* 'table' until he had matured and was known as a master. The group of men that he was slowly becoming associated with were more or less the original founding fathers of the magazine in 1841: John Tenniel, his old friend, Silver from Ipswich, John Leech whose work he had admired as a boy, Mark Lemon, the editor of immense girth, Horace Mayhew, Shirley Brooks and Percival Leigh. W.M. Thackeray was still loosely associated with this group but Dicky Doyle had left. All these men were 'Regency' in outlook, they belonged to a period before the Victorian era, a period of the 1830 revolutions when wit was more ribald and caricature more savage. Leech and Thackeray had tempered the heat of the fire

3.1 A party of musicians, 1865.
Pen and ink.
Dr Jonathan Fry.

3.2   The Artist's Mother, 1865–66.
         Pen, ink and bodycolour.   6³/₄ × 4¹/₄in.   17 × 11cm.
         Michael Broadbent Collection.

and given satire a more social dimension, but the dividing line was still marked.

Keene belonged to the second generation of *Punch* artists and writers, like du Maurier and Sambourne, more highly trained and more urbane than their predecessors. But with this attitude of mind the similarities ended. Keene remained an eccentric bachelor in a group of largely family men who kept up the trappings of Victorian life. He had no time for show or ceremony and yet he was much more of a traditionalist than any of them and far more politically to the right. His attitude to his colleagues was always therefore somewhat ambivalent, a non-political animal in an intensely partisan group, a loner among those who liked to do everything together. His friendships with those of the *Punch* table were never particularly close, preferring as he did the company of antiquarians and musicologists. During those famous dinners, when the main subject was the 'big cut' he seldom made a suggestion, in fact the conversations recorded in Henry Silver's diary rarely show a Keene comment. On the celebrated trips which the members of the table made together in the 1870s, Keene was a notable absentee, more at home in the seclusion of his untidy studio or at his cottage in rural Surrey.

And yet Keene owed so much to the magazine that gave him a home for nearly 40 years. It provided a safe and regular employment to somebody who was neither orderly nor business-like; it provided more or less congenial occupation in a gentlemanly atmosphere, and it gave him a clear sense of direction. Keene, like many of his artist friends, did not work best under pressure, hated deadlines and did not like to be trapped. *Punch* was a commercial venture but had fewer of the restraints of other popular magazines. Keene had disliked the *Illustrated London News* because of its topicality and scramble for illustrations, perhaps he would have found the discipline of novel illustrating similarly thwarting. In his *Punch* work he had the advantage of doing timeless illustrations that were not usually topical and in being able to choose his own stories and dialogue or adapt those of others. The big political cartoon in *Punch* was the only one that had to be topical and Keene was very rarely asked to draw it.

Tenniel left this impression of Keene at the *Punch* deliberations:

> For the first year or two he was a regular attendant, but afterwards came increasingly to look on what most consider an inestimable privilege as somewhat tiresome. As a matter of fact he was not very much use with suggestions for political cartoons and the general conduct of the paper, and the dinner was not of much use to him in providing his pencil with subjects. He spoke very little and was apt to throw cold water on projects under discussion. If specially appealed to for his opinion, he would, as likely as not, pass upon them a short and comprehensive criticism, such as 'D--d bad,' and relapse, with a twinkle in his eye, into smoke and silence.[1]

Keene can hardly have expected when he ate his first *Punch* dinner on 20 February 1860, that he would be succeeding John Leech in little over four years. Leech was only six years Keene's senior and gave great encouragement to the younger man, so that his premature death in October 1864 was both a great

3.3   Country Gentleman and gardener, *Punch*, 8 October 1870.
       Pen and ink.   4¼ × 7in.
       Chris Beetles, St James's Ltd.

3.4   Officers' Grievances, *Punch*, 20 December 1873.
       Pen and ink.   4¼ × 6½in.
       Chris Beetles, St James's Ltd.

3.5   A Note and Query, *Punch*, 21 June 1873.
      Pen and ink.   6³/₄ × 4¹/₄in.
      Chris Beetles, St James's Ltd.

3.6   Just in Time, *Punch Almanack*, 1879.
      Pen and ink.   10¹/₄ × 6³/₄in.   26 × 17cm.
      Michael Cook Collection.

tragedy and a great opportunity for Keene. Leech had prepared a ground of social and rural humour that had gained *Punch* much of its reputation. The sportsmen and country characters became part of the legacy for Keene, just as the drawing-room swells and affected hostesses were passed on to du Maurier. There was little for Keene to do in establishing this genre – it was all in place; all he had to concentrate on was perfecting his exquisite line and working out his method.

In that first period, when both Leech and Keene were working together, the latter's contributions are interesting. He was unable to utilise the socials that were Leech's province and so concentrated on a fairly limited repertoire of artist subjects, the volunteer movement and some juveniles. One has, for instance, on 11 February 1860 a youthful artist using his grandmother as model, probably Mrs Keene, both figures superbly conceived, then, on 14 April and 16 June 1860, wonderful volunteer illustrations. That spring he also uses his own studio in a splendid interior 'A Mere Trifle', published 10 March 1860, showing an unperturbed artist, himself, as the stove chimney catches on fire! This is such a truthful view of his artistic life – the old kettle on the hob and the dusty corners of the place – that none of his colleagues or his readers could have doubted his bohemianism. This subject, taking up one-third of a page, was not only larger than most socials but very new in its intense naturalism – certainly a fresh presence was making itself felt on *Punch*.

Keene's store continues to rise in 1861 and 1862, probably as a result of Leech's oil-painting exhibition that year and his illnesses. Keene was still confined to artists in their studios, the Royal Academy and the occasional omnibus scene as in that of 16 March 1861, with wonderful figures glimpsed from the rear. He is also developing the carefully modelled figure with great play in the folds of garments, the shading of backgrounds and natural light and shade, all quite exceptional in *Punch* until that time. Most of these subjects are unsigned, the occasional one, like that of 15 March 1862, being identified by the initials 'CK'.

The volumes for 1862 are important for they carry all three artists, Leech, Keene and George du Maurier, in a period of transition. Du Maurier's domestic scenes increase greatly in 1862–63 and both feature in the 'Mokeanna' parodies of March 1863. Keene has already advanced to some of the Leech territory in a partridge-shooting study of 24 September 1864 (Leech having gone abroad for his health). Just previous to this, in July, Keene had written to his friend Edwards, 'Leech is out of town & the Punch People are very exigent to think of a subject for me.'[2] Immediately after John Leech's death in October 1864, Keene contributed large subjects, signed by 'CK', and succeeded to the street, field and railway incidents of his great predecessor.

Keene's somewhat taciturn approach to his colleagues was merely the symptom of an incredible dedication to this task. He did not value any time spent away from his studio if it was not to collect information for his drawings; his hobbies of

3.7   Transpositions, *Punch*, 1884.
Pen and ink.   8½ × 5½in.   21.4 × 14.1cm.
Michael Cook Collection.

3.8 Oxford and Cambridge Boat Race, *c.* 1880.
Pen and ink. 5 × 7in. 13 × 18cm.
Michael Broadbent Collection.

walking, playing the bagpipes and antiquarianism supplied him with subjects. 'Draw a thing as you see it!' was his invariable reply when questioned about his methods and his great dictum about art was 'If a man can draw, he can draw anything!'[3] The ever-observant du Maurier records Keene's obsessive concern for studying from life. While he had a studio in the West End, Keene frequently dined at Pamphillon's off Oxford Circus. Du Maurier wrote in January 1862:

> Marks comes a great deal to Pamphillon's … Old Keene always there of course as usual, with his regular joint, College pudding, two pats of butter, glass of porter, coffee & 3 pipes; after which bonsoir la compagnie, nothing shall prevent him from going to his work at the Langham.[4]

Keene's reluctance to discuss aesthetics did not mean that he had no theories and, in fact, his methods were complex. Most of the time that he was serving on *Punch*, his work was engraved by Swain, one of the leading wood engravers of the day. Swain has left his impressions of the artist's work and how difficult it was to interpret. Keene experimented by making his own inks, by using improvised pens, sometimes a pointed piece of wood lashed to a pen-holder, and was notorious for working on odd scraps of paper. Swain wrote in 1892:

> … he had the strongest aversion to drawing-paper or Bristol boards, preferring any scrap, even half a sheet of note-paper, with a rough grain and coloured by age. He would often put in a slight wash and then work over it with ink or chalk, and sometimes pencil. In fact, it was impossible for any one unacquainted with his method to ascertain the means by which he obtained his effects.[5]

His improvised pens together with the greyish inks enabled him to create 'soft touches' and 'delicate shades of expression' which no standard product could imitate and no engraver transcribe. Some idea of the close work Keene engaged in and the conditions in which he drew can be appreciated from the marvellous ink drawing of about 1860, 'Two Artists Working By Lamplight in a Studio' (now in the Tate Gallery). (See Plate 2.6, p. 26.) This is probably of Keene's friends Rossiter and Hayes. Although not intended for illustration, this carefully graded drawing would have been impossible for the engraver to visualise.

The subscribers of *Punch* obtained an adequate image of what Keene had intended but without any of the subtle effects and brilliant shadings that Keene loved – everything was reduced to the uncompromising blackness of printer's ink. This is abundantly clear from the contrast between the great studio interior of 14 February 1863, now in the British Museum, and its appearance on the page. The former is grainy but well defined, the latter darkened beyond belief. But the readers were not primarily fine-art experts and were satisfied with the engravings as charming vehicles for wit. For Keene and the handful of serious collectors who knew his original drawings, the contrast must have been devastating.

Keene was also an excellent portraitist, as the Tate Gallery self-portrait and numerous other studies testify. The accuracy of the self-portrait can be judged with the photograph by Harral of about 1865 (see Frontispiece) and many other smaller studies on the backs of envelopes exist. His sketches of friends at the Langham are well developed and his hasty sketches of two celebrated contemporaries, D.G. Rossetti and William Morris (see Plate 2.7, p. 26), are among the most telling of their kind. It is therefore strange that this talent was not utilised more in *Punch*, a useful asset in the cartoonist's armoury and a valuable insight into character. He seems not to have succeeded with portraiture if the intention was to be funny. Shirley Brooks records on 13 September 1869, 'The cut of me was a treachery',[6] and Layard adds that it was hardly a passable likeness! Keene was not a caricaturist and was not roused on most political issues, he was too fond of frail humanity to inject the necessary venom into these works. His first attempt, late in 1854, 'Austria Defies Russia' is not very strong and later ones were done under protest. Mark Lemon occasionally asked him to do a full-page picture to face Tenniel's cartoon but actual cartoon work was rare. In October 1878, he was forced to stand in for Tenniel but could not rid himself of the uncongenial task quickly enough.

If he was not a political cartoonist and had to some extent inherited a social genre from Leech, what was most original about his subjects from the 1860s to the 1880s? He certainly created a *dramatis personae* of his own, neither borrowed from the hunting fields of Leech nor the drawing-rooms of du Maurier, neither of which he frequented. Spielmann, the first historian of *Punch*, refers to the range of characters:

> ... the Kirk Elder, the slavey, the policeman, the fussy City man, the diner-out, the waiter, the cabman, the henpecked husband, the drunkard, the gillie, the Irish peasant, the schoolboy, and the Mrs. Brown of Arthur Sketchley's prosaic muse.[7]

Keene was not an inventor of comic types but an observer of the humour in humanity which he saw around him. Joseph Pennell grasps this very well when he was asked to look through Keene's life studies after his death:

> Each is a distinct impression – for if anyone was an impressionist it was Charles Keene – of the flabby, or fat, or tired, or swaggering, or bored model, before him. He used the same models over and over again, one of them it is amusing to see, a woman of the type drawn repeatedly by Etty and Mulready; a plump, heavy, ungraceful, clumsy sort of female animal, sagging and flopping and sprawling about – the real early Victorian woman, innocent of all elegance and grace and distinction. She must have sagged and flopped and sprawled when she posed for Etty and Mulready, but in their work is little to show, whether or no, they saw that she did. There is no mistaking that Keene did see her as she was, not as he fancied she would look well, on paper and canvas. Critics who say that Keene could not draw a lady or a beautiful face, meaning that he did not draw conventional fashion plates, will turn to these life studies as additional proof.[8]

In the early part of 1863, Keene moved from the old Langham sheds in Clipstone Street to a studio above Elliott & Fry's photographic business at 55 Baker Street. It may have been his better financial position on *Punch* that enabled this move. He did not receive a salary from the magazine like most of his fellow artists, preferring payment for each drawing. From 1865 he was involved in producing the coloured frontispieces for the *Punch* 'Pocket Books', delightful leather-bound diaries which were packed with information and also small wood engravings. The folding frontispieces were actually etched on steel and this may have been the cause of Keene's entry into etched work, dealt with in a later chapter. He designed 17 of the *Punch* 'Pocket Books' from 1865 to 1881, racking his brains for new ideas as the autumn approached. They were often unlike his normal work, being elongated and very concentrated in content, the dialogue contained in balloons issuing from the mouths of the principal figures. The design also had to contain a title-page with a portrait of Mr Punch, different on each occasion.

His first *Pocket Book* had a humorous look at table-rapping, 'Punch's Spirit Lamp', in which select ladies and gentleman are appalled by a piece of levitation. More typical is the *Pocket Book* for 1867 where he depicts 'The Matrimonial Arrangement Association', a sort of Victorian dating agency with prospective customers leaning over a counter to examine daguerrotypes! The books could not contain any allusions that were likely to date between conception and publication, so matrimonial and social matters were easier. These ideas continue in 1870 and 1871 with 'The Ladies' New Gallery' in the House of Commons and 'Gallant Rescue Off The Bachelor Rocks' accompanied by a facetious report with the sub-title 'Man The Wife-Boat'. In 1872 he had 'The Matrimonial Hurlingham' shooting down prospective husbands, and in 1873, 'Science in her Silver Slippers', a parody on the Victorian ladies' fascination for clever old men. Similar themes continue in 1875 with 'The Androgynaeum Club', and in 1876 with 'The Modern Babylonian Marriage Mart'. The last five issues were wood engravings coloured by hand and altogether a coarser feature than in the earlier books. Two original drawings for these illustrations exist, one in the British Museum Collection and another in a private collection.

The *Punch Almanack* was a supplement to *Punch* that appeared at the start of the new year and this was heavily illustrated, often by one artist. Keene felt very harassed by these deadlines and commented in a letter to Edwards on 27 October 1867, 'You don't know what it is to have to do with Publishers just before Christmas'.[9]

Forrest Reid talks of the two styles of Keene in the early 1860s, his '*Once a Week* manner' where he was 'working in the direct tradition of the 'sixties' and 'the freer style of his *Punch* work'.[10] It would be more correct to say that there were four styles in Keene's development: the early phase of the 1840s and 1850s when he was working in the manner of Stothard and Harvey, the years from 1855 to 1865 when he was influenced by the Pre-Raphaelites, the mature period of 1865 to 1880 and the final burst of energy and creativity from 1880 to 1890. It is perfectly true that his drawings for *Once a Week* and his drawings for *Punch* are stylistically different, the first requiring a more serious slant and the second usually light-hearted, but they are both acute pieces of observation and sensitivity.

One of the problems in looking at Keene's *Punch* work before 1879 is the absence of many finished drawings. A few, like the artist in his studio, may have been re-drawn for a friend, but most were drawn on to the block for engraving. Keene was one of the old school of artists who had served their apprenticeship in a wood-engraving establishment and were trained for book illustration. When Chatto produced his important book *History of Wood-Engraving* in 1861, he listed Keene among those artists who actually engraved as distinct from painters and draughtsmen. By 1870, with the advent of art schools, they were a diminishing band.

Like his friend Tenniel, Keene was expected to discuss a subject with *Punch* and make his finished drawing on the block for delivery on the Friday night. Then the block would be engraved in sections by one or two engravers by Saturday night and handed to the printers in readiness for its appearance the following week. That he had many studies in hand and a portfolio from which to extract ideas is evident from the numerous surviving scraps and the existence of at least three sketch-books, one in the Victoria & Albert Museum and two in the Pierpont Morgan Library. His method of using friends for ideas is dealt with in the next chapter.

Many of the earlier illustrations for *Punch* are only seen through the studies and tracings that remain after the original finished work had been cut away. There are a number of existing studies of the early 1860s done on thin paper ready to transfer to the block and some are illustrated here (see Plate 2.8, p. 29). One gets from these a slight indication of the refinement of Keene's line and the virtual impossibility of translating such delicate images on to the printed page. Even if Swain's men performed a miracle, the block still had to go through the turmoil of the printing press where tones on the paper were produced by putting pressure on certain parts of the block. Added to this, it was always difficult to get an even printing when the blocks were chased in with the letterpress: see, for example, Plate 4.2, p. 70. Keene's comments on Bewick could equally be applied to himself; he said of that artist that he 'worked in and was hampered by an ungrateful material'.[11]

The invention in 1872 of a method of photographing the drawing on to the block from a stiff paper changed all this. It enabled the work to be done more quickly and it enabled the artist to retain the original drawing, which he was at liberty to sell. We know in the case of Tenniel, that he had previously developed a kind of short-hand with Swain so that the drawing on the block was not a finished one. This relieved the hard-pressed Tenniel from doing a finished drawing at all.[12] It is therefore small wonder that he resisted the new technique where a highly worked drawing had to be completed for the photography. It may have been that Keene, another older artist felt the same. Neither of them adapted to the new method quickly, Keene not before 1878–79 and Tenniel not till 1890! Keene was far too unworldly to sell his completed drawings and never seems to have realised their value except as presents.

For Keene, the change-over must have come in the first months of 1879. I have his preliminary sketch for one of his Irish subjects 'The Saxon Oppressor' which is squared up for transferring to the wood-block and this is dated 2 February 1878. After this date there are a vast range of finished drawings by Keene which improve year by year towards the mid-1880s (see Plates 3.15, p. 65 and 4.5, p. 79).

Pennell states in *Work of Charles Keene* that the artist changed his style to accommodate the poor engraving in *Punch*. Describing Keene's work he writes:

> It was exquisitely delicate, wonderfully refined; it depended for its beauty either upon one line rightly placed, or a multitude of lines so subtle, so close, that the brutal point of a graver in the hands of an ordinary man could never penetrate their interstices ... Keene's style of drawing became bolder and bolder as time went on. For his own pleasure he continued to make, with his pen, little masterpieces, which in their refinement are worthy to rank with the etchings of Rembrandt and Whistler. In his studies, and he made innumerable studies for *Punch* pictures, he never varied his handling. But when working for *Punch* he either began to think more about the engraver, or else despaired of him and gave him up as hopeless.[13]

By 1866, he had abandoned the meticulous care of the *Once a Week* drawings for a more generalised style suitable to the magazine. Pennell comments:

> Instead of the elaborate cross-hatching by which the modelling and the fleshy look of his faces was obtained, short straight lines have been substituted, and a more open cross-hatching in the background, in striking contrast to the delicate, beautiful, tender studies, impossible to reproduce, made by him for the finished illustrations.[14]

He cites the study for 'Lesson In Perspective', one of his most sensitive works (see Plate 2.19, p. 43) and its reproduction in the *Punch Almanack* for 1868.

He was able at self-portraiture and a number of illustrations contain his gaunt figure, never a caricature, simply true to life. He depicts himself in the illustration of 'McClanky' and his bagpipes, in the series 'Englishmen in Brittany' and most famously of all, in 1882, 'The Man That Hath Not Music,' (see Plate 3.10, p. 59). Here the irrepressible musician, which Keene certainly was, stands over his subdued friend and offers to play upon the bagpipes once again!

During the 1870s, Keene's range of subject also broadened to suit a changing public. He drew a number of Irish scenes in January 1874 (although it is not recorded that he ever went there), and was topical enough to include early bicycles ('More Economy', 3 January 1874), cricket, tennis and omnibuses. His urchins and flunkeys were rather an inheritance from John Leech, especially the splendid 'Otium Cum', from 28 March 1874.

Pennell, referring to a Keene drawing of three years later, writes, 'Keene at this time, 1877, had not begun to set the engraver the impossible tasks of his later years.' These drawings, leading up to the years of his death are the most amazing and magical ones he ever did, atmospheric, moody and quite without parallel in

3.9   Triumphs of Art, 22 May 1880.
       Pen and ink.   5 × 4in.
       Chris Beetles, St James's Ltd.

3.10   The Man That Hath Not Music, Self-Portrait, 1882.
        Pen and ink.   8¹/₂ × 5¹/₄in.   21.5 × 13.5cm.
        Michael Broadbent Collection.

British illustration. From the early 1880s there is a richness and a tonality by which Keene injects 'colour' and texture into his pictures with the brilliance of his hatching and the subtle uses of sepia, grey and vermilion inks. Notable among these are the parade ground scene (see Plate 3.12, p. 62), an interview in a library (the glazed shelving given an extraordinary three-dimensional quality with its skilfully grained lines: Plate 3.7, p. 52), and the policeman and the diner out (see Plate 3.14, p. 64). This last, dating from 1884, gives a clear idea where Keene was going; it is a real life subject worthy of Forain and more French than English. It would be impossible to interpret by wood engraving the complex darks and lights in this sketch, the sophistication of the modelling of costume and physical space, let alone the beam from the policeman's torch.

During the 1880s, Keene's output remained constant but the work, even in the wood engravings, was more painterly and vigorous in approach. One thinks particularly of 'Division' (31 January 1885), the boldness of 'Camel Ship' (14 March 1885) (see Plate 3.11, p. 61), 'The Fitness of Things' in the *Almanack* for 1885, to mention a few. He was tackling a number of more social subjects and even borrowed the aesthetic mould of du Maurier on one occasion. Some of the illustrations are three-quarter page size, a format that he had used in earlier days. In his 'Hyperbole (4 April 1885), he depicts a rear view of men in top hats almost prefiguring the idioms of Phil May.

Keene's last few years produced drawings of an impressionistic brilliance and artistic shorthand that would defy any engraver. They seem concerned with atmosphere and tones and the subtleties of extracting 'colour' out of his limited palette of brown and vermilion inks and their effects on a variety of papers. He seemed to be moving closer and closer to the French ideal of a synthesis of light and shade, and away from the concept of modelling form. Some contemporary writers likened him to Forain and in his last *Punch* contribution, for 16 August 1890, ''Arry On The Boulevards' the connection is apt (see Plate 3.16, p. 66). This evocative sketch comes out well on the printed page as a memorable contribution to the *fin d siècle*. ''Arry', the invention of the *Punch* writer E.J. Milliken, was a type of Victorian cad or 'masher' who journeyed through various picaresque adventures. It says something for the 67-year-old artist that he was able to keep abreast of both social and artistic developments. We know from an unpublished letter to F.G. Burnand that the drawings were made in 1889 when Keene was too ill to cross to France. He writes, 'I've done two drawings of 'Arry as you suggested but please be less vague about these subjects. I forget all about Paris so long since I was there ...'[15] Pennell shows the whole sequence of this illustration: first a rather broad sketch of the whole Parisian street after dark, the light shining out from the street café; then a sketch in coloured inks of the subject more constricted in composition, the character of 'Arry more developed and the gas lamps and penumbra more marked. The printed version has more contrast but

3.11 Camel Ship, *Punch*, 1885.
Pen and ink.   6 × 8in.   15 × 20.5cm.
Michael Broadbent Collection.

3.12 The Commissariat, *Punch Almanack*, 1879.
Pen and ink.   11½ x 7¼in.   29.4 x 18.6cm.
Michael Cook Collection.

3.13   The British Drama, *Punch*, 1883.
Pen and ink.   5½ × 9in.   14 × 23cm.
Michael Cook Collection.

3.14 Diner Out and Policeman, *Punch*, 19 January 1884.
Pen and ink.   5 x 7³/₄in.   12.8 x 19.7cm.
Michael Cook Collection.

3.15　The Irrepressible, *Punch*, 1886.
Pen and ink.　5¼ × 8in.　13.5 × 20.5cm.
Michael Broadbent Collection.

3.16   'Arry On The Boulevards, *Punch*, 1890.
       Pen and ink and wash.   7¹/₂ × 4in.
       Michael Broadbent Collection.

rather lacks the free spirit of the ink version. The first sketch has the freedom of a Toulouse-Lautrec and is quite remarkable; the second has more the individuality of a Forain or the animation of a Steinlen. Lord Clark may have been thinking of this work when he wrote, 'At no point do we feel that he has betrayed or corrupted his talent, he is perhaps the only English artist whose work improved to the last.'[16]

NOTES

1. Layard, 1892, p. 76.
2. Fitzwilliam MSS 5, Keene.
3. Layard, 1892, p. 144.
4. Du Maurier, 1951, p. 118.
5. Layard, 1892, p. 144.
6. Diary, London Library.
7. Spielmann, 1895, p. 489.
8. Pennell, 1897b, p. 18.
9. Fitzwilliam MSS 19, Keene.
10. *Print Collectors Quarterly*, 17, p. 40.
11. Layard, 1892, p. 230.
12. Engen, 1991, p. 102.
13. Pennell, 1897b, pp. 30–31.
14. ibid., pp. 30–1.
15. Private Collection.
16. Arts Council, 1952, p. 8.

3.17   Physicians and Invalid by Joseph Crawhall (1821–1896). Dated 7 May 1880.
Pen and watercolour.   Album 12 x 9³/₄in.
Cyril Fry Collection.

4 Observer or humorist?

For all his bohemianism and eccentricity, Charles Keene was most at home in a
civilised circle of artists and writers. He was acquainted with most of the
celebrated draughtsmen of his time and was on good terms with many of them. As
we shall see, he was to become a part of the Birket Foster colony at Witley, Surrey,
although he claimed to keep these ardent country-house dwellers at a reasonable
distance! As he was already established when such figures as James McNeill
Whistler and George du Maurier came to London, he was regarded by them with
a certain awe. He knew both D.G. Rossetti and William Morris, though not well,

4.1   Rallying, *Punch*, 4 November 1882.
Pen and brown ink.   8¹/₂ x 5¹/₄in.   21.3 x 13.5cm.
Michael Cook Collection.

"RALLYING."

Doctor (sotto voce to his Colleague). "We must reduce the Fever and abate the Thirst!"
Patient (who had overheard). "If you'll redooce the Fever, Gen'lemen—I'll uld'take—to abate the Thirst myshelf!!"

4.2   Rallying, Wood engraving for *Punch*, 4 November 1882.

and hovered on the edge of the later Pre-Raphaelite circle, striking up friendships with Holman Hunt and Millais in the 1860s. The truth was that he preferred the company of the minor artists and literati of the time, gentleman painters like himself, scholars with a taste for archaeology and antiquarianism and amateurs from the merchant class, who painted a little and etched a lot. The one exception to this rule was Edward Fitzgerald, the translator and poet with whom he had a warm friendship; Keene was innocently unaware of Fitzgerald's true standing as a poet.

Thoughtful and monosyllabic, Keene liked the convivial gatherings of like-minded men, whether at Moray Lodge, the home of Arthur Lewis, at the Tulse Hill mansion of the Ionides or at the Arts Club. The latter became a very favourite haunt and the letters between him and Edwin Edwards show how often he was there between the 1860s and 1880s. He usually found some anecdote of the Arts to pass on to his friends and he groaned inwardly if the Club was closed during the summer months or vacated by his friends during the season.

Keene was essentially an observer, in both public and private life. How else could he have built up that masterly grasp of character, the slightest expressions, the minute inflections of eye and mouth, the wave of a disdainful hand, the weight of the body intently listening or lolling back in reflection? Keene's clubbable personality was at its best as listener or the amused observer of other men's foibles. He recounts with zest the frolics of his fellow members, the perfect reporter in word as in line. ' … there has been a row there,' he reports to Edwards on 23 July 1869,

> little Swinburne misbehaved himself there the other day he was drunk & stamped on the members hats & knocked somebody's pipe out of his mouth & the Committee were very much put out, & requested him to leave & threatened a General Meeting. However Jemmy [Whistler] stood up for him & saw the Executive the other night & talked 'em over & got the poor little wretch out of his mess …[1]

He was also the perpetrator of a mock epistle to Edwin Edwards 'got up' at the Club over a dispute as to the meaning of 'Corbie Stepped Gables'. Keene made a diagram of a gabled house with a corbie sitting on each step! This document is signed solemnly by William Burges, the Gothic architect, William Seddon, the architect and George Aitchison, Professor of Architecture at the Royal Academy. Keene, the Chelsea bohemian, moved with ease in such circles.

Keene was unusual among his brothers of the pencil in being an excellent letter-writer and a very literary man. His descriptions of sleeping in a first-class railway compartment *en route* for Scotland or being lost in the lanes of Suffolk are amusing incidents, told with precision and clarity. It was this narrative style that he was able to bring to the situations he recorded in his *Punch* drawings, crafting the dialogue as carefully as if it had been part of a stage play. Keene was immensely proud of his 'legends' as he called them. Forrest Reid in his well-known study *Illustrators of*

The Sixties takes up this point:

> If a word is altered, if even a letter is altered in his dialect jokes, he is furious. He is so careful of them that, distrustful of his handwriting, he frequently prints the words, thus leaving no excuse for inaccuracy. Bitter is his anger when the 'sapient editor' tampers with his text.[2]

This tampering with the legends happened many times and brought down the ire of Keene on his editors. But equally often the subjects suggested were considered *risqué* or indelicate, he mentions one of these to Mrs Edwards concerning earthworms conversing in a graveyard and Layard records another where one widow says to another of the deceased 'I know where he passes his evenings now!'[3]

Reid also takes issue with Keene's biographer G.S. Layard over the originality of Keene's humour which later critics felt was acquired. Almost all the great artists of the popular press, seeking out subjects for weekly publications, relied to some extent on their friends or on fortunate aids to memory. The *Punch* artists were especially desperate for material, John Leech and Tenniel receiving inspiration from others, just as the Pre-Raphaelites had copied from each other. Keene's repertoire of character studies required accompanying dialogue and Keene was far-reaching in using friends' subjects while being open and generous in acknowledging them.

He was only unusual in the fact that he was prepared to gather 'material' from fellow artists such as Birket Foster, A.W. Cooper, Stacy Marks, Robert Dudley and Edwin Edwards, the amateur whom he had got to know in the 1860s. In July 1864, Keene writes to Edwards, 'Leech is out of town and the "Punch" people are very exigent. Try and think of a subject for me!'[4] This constant pressure must have been very trying, particularly as the 'socials' as opposed to the 'politicals' were not discussed at the *Punch* table and therefore the full onus for them fell upon the artist.

From his earliest connection with the magazine he had relied on the good offices of friends, and indeed Captain Robley of the 91st Highlanders regularly supplied him with jokes and these were marked 'R'. Keene never tried to pretend that other men's inspirations were his own. One illustration, on 28 November 1885, was supplied by Farrar Ranson, the mayor of Norwich and another, on 3 August 1889, was suggested to him by Stacy Marks and includes a very good portrait of the academician with artist's hat and umbrella!

A more consistent contributor was Andrew Tuer, the publisher and amateur of the arts who began to send Keene 'legends' in about 1882. According to Tuer, there was a tacit understanding that any works that were used and published in *Punch* would be paid for with the gift of the original drawing to Tuer. Neither party seemed to be aware that the ink drawings, after they had been used, were of any specific value. This arrangement lasted for some years until Keene was prompted by friends to consider his drawings as valuable and part of his stock in trade. In the early part of 1884, the flow of gifts ceased and Tuer immediately wrote to Keene. Keene replied:

> Dear Tuer, Let us have an understanding. These original drawings are my poor 'stock in trade' – my capital – my copyrights, etc. Do you wish to purchase this sketch as a matter of business? If you want a replica of this in particular I'll make one and give it you with pleasure in this case, but I can't undertake to do it always.[5]

Tuer, embarrassed that he should be thought grasping, immediately replied to his friend:

> I always understood – how I got it into my stupid old head I do not know – that you considered an original contribution that you could accept for 'Punch' as a quid pro quo for your original sketch. I don't think that I was even aware at first that you ever disposed of your drawings. I simply felt proud to possess your drawings of my little jokes. On looking over the sketches that I have, I find that I supplied matter for all except three –.

Keene concluded the correspondence amicably by saying, 'You ought to see them before you take them, and I'll forward them to you if you like them, and I ask five guineas each if you take them.'[6]

J.W. Barnes, F.S.A., of Durham, a fellow Bewick enthusiast also supplied Keene with subjects. As with the case of A.W. Cooper he kept an album of Keene's work which must have been long since dispersed. In 1888, Barnes supplied Keene with a story about a squire and a northern farmer, fresh from the moors of his native Durham. Keene was in the habit of rewarding this friend with the finished drawings and sent this one at Christmas 1888 with an accompanying letter: 'Did you see the cut in Punch of the sporting story you gave me, I'm sending you this sketch (a Christmas card if you won't mind its having appeared in Punch).'[7] The sketch has been lightly coloured in crayon by Keene to make it more seasonal, a highly unusual embellishment. Barnes in return used to send Keene presents of woodcock, grouse and teal.

The view from the editorial chair, as expressed by F.G. Burnand was rather different:

> Charles Keene used to be supplied by some joke purveyor with little memorandum books full of coloured sketches (years after my first joining he showed me several of them) roughly illustrating jokes which were to supply him with material. The consequence of this was that, as Keene drew much from his own immediate observation, the collection of jokes became stale, and many of them had been repeated on 'change (the great joke mart) and in clubs before Charles made selections from the stock, for which I believe, he regularly paid the purveyor.[8]

This was a distortion of Keene's genius as an observer and a distiller of what he saw around him and it also rather passes over one of the most surprising partnerships of the nineteenth century, that between Charles Keene and Joseph Crawhall.

Joseph Crawhall (1821–96) was a Newcastle businessman and rope-maker with sporting and antiquarian inclinations. Coming from the Northumbrian heartland, where wood engraving had reached its zenith in the hands of Thomas Bewick and his followers, it is not surprising that Crawhall began to turn his eyes away from business and towards art in the 1850s. He was particularly fascinated by old books, old woodcuts and Northumbrian lore and he combined all these in his first publication, *The Compleatest Angling Booke* which he had printed in 1859. This quaint collection of fishing tales imitated the old chapbooks and pre-dated an interest that would later come into vogue. The book's 40 copies were for private distribution and were followed by an extract, separately printed, *Ye louing ballad of Lorde Bateman To itte's own Tune herin sette fforth* (1860), in an edition of 15 copies. These were succeeded by more venturous collections, *A Collection of Right Merrie Garlands* (1864), and *Chaplets from Coquet-side* (1873).

This combination of slightly zany antiquarianism and music was bound to attract the notice of Charles Keene, and a mutual friend had the stroke of genius to bring these two eccentrics together. Mr Henry Shield had noticed that Crawhall kept an album of amusing incidents to which he added as they occurred to him. They were presumably for use in his publications, but Shield thought they could be of service to Keene and an introduction was arranged in 1872. Keene's impressions of Crawhall's collection after a first visit are rapturous:

> You'd have liked his house, crammed full of curios, and of the best. On his walls the rarest prints and etchings, etc. – and he knows all about them, too – a few pictures and drawings, several oil pictures of Blacklock's, and no end of books, armour, arms, and any amount of Pots and Plates of his own painting … C. is a great smoker, and gets up every morning at four, comes down and has a pipe and does an hour's work (painting), and then goes to bed again![9]

It was hardly likely that such a meeting of minds could be anything other than fruitful!

If there was a swopping of ideas for *Punch* subjects in the early days, for example, 'A Narrow Escape' (6 September 1873), and 'Happy Thought' (16 December 1876), things got on to a more formal basis in 1877. In that year Keene wrote to his Northumbrian friend:

> Dear Mr Crawhall, many thanks for the loan of the sketch-books. I enjoyed them again and again with renewed chucklings, but what a mouth-watering larder to lay open to a ravenous joke-seeker! Mayn't I have one for 'Punch'? If I don't have a prohibitory postcard (which I hope you won't hesitate to send me if you've the slightest objection), I can't choose but make free![10]

Crawhall's albums, which are today in public and private collections, have his drawings mounted on card pages with the Keene wood engraving for *Punch* alongside. Crawhall often mounted Keene's letters in these books and one that I have seen has the following inscription by Crawhall on its title-page:

> The legends, texts, or descriptive matters appended to the following engravings from 'Punch' were sent, as imagined, invented, acquired, or occurred, to my friend Charles S. Keene, over a period of 18 years, and on such data the annexed translations are founded; The Albums referred to in his letter containing my rough sketches were returned to me during his last illness & are now

in my possession. Joseph Crawhall, 12 Eldon Square ... Newcastle on Tyne ... 2 Sydenham Terrace – Ealing London W Since 23 April 1890.[11]

Crawhall's wit and humour were to supply Keene with some 250 illustrations between 1873 and 1890, an astonishing record. Keene's influence may well have been responsible for getting his Newcastle friend a much wider public, for an introduction to Tuer meant that Crawhall's strange compilations of verse and woodcuts were published by Andrew Tuer from his Leadenhall Press. These included *Border Notes & Mixty-Maxty* (1880) dedicated to Charles Keene, *Chap-Book Chaplets* (1883), *Olde Tayles Newlye Related* and *Olde ffrendes wyth newe faces* (1883). Crawhall's sense of design would have appealed to Keene and the London-based artist was sensitive to artistic changes. The beginnings of an Arts and Crafts revival was stirring and these simple books with their hand-colouring would have appealed to a new sophisticated audience tired of Victorian industrialised book production. Keene himself would just have enjoyed the fun of the whole thing.

The Keene and Crawhall friendship was extremely fruitful but it was also quite different from that with Andrew Tuer. There was no question of a disagreement over the arrangements or a request for five guineas for drawings – one is forced to ask why this was the case. It is only necessary to look at a few examples in the Crawhall albums to understand why Charles Keene felt so indebted to this eccentric Northumbrian antiquary. Many of the sketches supplied by Crawhall to Keene not only have their legends and situations copied by the artist but their compositions as well.

In his *Punch* illustration 'A Blank Day' (1880), Keene depicts a disenchanted fisherman alighting from a railway carriage having caught nothing. The album sketch by Crawhall, dated 18 June 1880 has a remarkably similar scene; all the main characters are in the same positions and even the hands of the disillusioned sportsman depicted in the same way. Crawhall, though an amateur, could show expression admirably. Similar comparisons can be made with 'Contumacious', a court scene in which an old lag of a poacher is facing the magistrates. Crawhall's sketch, dated 19 May 1880, is rough and ready and spirited; Keene's illustration from it is a masterly interpretation, but the spirit is the same. The prisoner in the dock stares out in the same way with the policeman behind him, only the positions of the magistrates and solicitors are slightly altered.

Two further examples illustrated here make the point again. In 'Optics' a scene of a slide lecture and a rural audience, Crawhall presents a short-sighted lecturer, a be-hatted audience and an old crone in one corner (see Plate 4.3, p. 76). This is dated 17 July 1880, some ten months before Keene's version appeared in *Punch* (see Plate 4.4, p. 77). Keene has turned the lecturer slightly to the left but he remains a similar figure; the audience are more defined but the old lady remains in the same place. In 'Rallying', in the *Punch* of 4 November 1882, Keene uses a

4.3   Optics by Joseph Crawhall (1821–1896). Dated 17 July 1880.
Pen and watercolour.   Album 12 × 9¾in.
Cyril Fry Collection.

"OPTICS."

Lecturer. "NOW LET ANYONE GAZE STEADFASTLY ON ANY OBJECT—SAY, FOR INSTANCE, HIS WIFE'S EYE—AND HE'LL SEE HIMSELF LOOKING SO EXCEEDINGLY SMALL, THAT——"
Strong-minded Lady (in Front Row). "HEAR! HEAR! HEAR!"

4.4   Optics, Wood engraving for *Punch*, 21 May 1881.

subject drawn out by Crawhall two years previously on 7 May 1880 (see Plates 4.1 & 4.2, pp. 69 and 70). The composition is reversed (indeed as it would have been on a woodblock, a process that was second nature to Keene) but the expressions of the figures are essentially Crawhall's. The ailing man in the chair retains all the torpor of Crawhall's sketch, and the two physicians stand in poses that are reminiscent of the album drawing.

This discovery in no way diminishes Keene's stature as an artist or an observer of nature. He took the germ of an idea and expanded it with his masterly line and intuitive understanding of form and character. As Keene's earlier editor Shirley Brooks observed, 'Charles Keene never laid a line down without being sure that it conveyed his exact meaning.'[12]

The partnership was not always strong enough to combat editorial disapproval or misunderstanding and Keene felt duty-bound to apologise to his begetter as a humorist for such shortcomings. In *Punch's Almanack* for 1880, Crawhall provided the subject of a Scotch Field Preacher vociferating in broad dialect. When Tom Taylor, the editor, altered the words to make them more comprehensible to an English readership, Keene was furious. He wrote to Crawhall, 'When I saw the Almanack I was in a great rage that they had altered your legend in the drawing of the Scotch preacher, and wrote instanter to the sapient editor. I enclose copy. I'll never forgive him.'[13]

It was Keene's contemporary on *Punch*, George du Maurier, who survived him for a number of years, who was best able to put his art into the context of humour and satire. Du Maurier states in his book *Social Pictorial Satire* (1898) that Keene was no satirist: 'His nature was too tolerant and too sweet for hate, and that makes him a bad and somewhat perfunctory hater.'[14] Du Maurier adds that Keene's *dramatis personae* are not types (the usual source of humorous portraiture), 'they are characters themselves rather than types of English characters.'[15] Keene was actually much better at observing the individual rather than the general in humankind, the natural preserve of the serious artist.

Du Maurier in his book, treats Keene as a great draughtsman rather than a great humorist:

> Among his other gifts he had a physical gift of inestimable value for such work as ours – namely, a splendid hand – a large, muscular, well-shaped, and most workman-like hand, whose long deft fingers could move with equal ease and certainty in all directions. I have seen it at work – and it was a pleasure to watch its acrobatic dexterity, its unerring precision of touch. It could draw with nonchalant facility parallel straight lines, or curved, of just the right thickness and distance from each other – almost as regular as if they had been drawn with a ruler or compass – almost, but not *quite*. The quiteness would have made them mechanical, and robbed them of their charm of human handicraft. A cunning and obedient slave, this wonderful hand, for which no command from the head could come amiss – a slave, moreover, that had most thoroughly learned its business by long apprenticeship to one special trade, like the head and like the eye that guided it.[16]

4.5 By Proxy, *Punch*, 7 October 1882. One of the subjects supplied by Crawhall.
Pen and ink.   6 × 8in.   15 × 22cm.
Michael Cook Collection.

4.6 Cantankerous, *Punch*, 30 September 1882. Inscribed from Keene to Crawhall 27 October 1882.
Pen and ink.   7 × 10in.   18 × 25.5cm.
Michael Broadbent Collection.

80

Pennell makes the point that Keene's work was accepted with 'general indifference' by all except the *cognoscenti* among artists and writers. 'I need not point out,' he writes in 1897, 'how small a fraction of the popularity of the *Punch* artists fell to him. To the many, *Punch* meant Leech or Doyle or du Maurier; only the few looked to it for Keene.'[17] This is certainly borne out by the scarcity of the collected edition of his work *Our People*. This was published by Bradbury, Agnew & Co. in 1881, when the artist was at the height of his powers, and it certainly gives the best cross-section of his work to be found anywhere. It contains 404 wood engravings by Swain and is in handsome folio form. A smaller American edition was published by Osgood of Boston. The only comparable volumes by *Punch* artists are the three landscape volumes *Pictures of Life and Character* by John Leech, and *Society Pictures* by George du Maurier. Both of these are found in considerable quantities today whereas *Our People* is seldom seen. The print run of Keene's book must have been appreciably smaller, the works of the other two being household names in Victorian England and their draughtsmanship essentially amusing.

Layard was able to record in 1892 that *Our People* was

> … not a mere picture-book. Opening its pages is like opening a series of windows and finding Nature herself informed and animated by her best spirit of unexaggerated fun. Where Keene attempted to be more humorous than his mistress – and this was always against the grain – he signally failed.[18]

The humour was the synthesis of observation and not of exaggeration, a point that du Maurier developed in writing of the Keene line:

> His mere pen-strokes have, for the expert, a beauty and an interest quite apart from the thing they are made to depict, whether he uses them as mere outlines to express the shape of things animate or inanimate, even such shapeless, irregular things as the stones on a sea-beach – or in combination to suggest the tone and colour of a dress-coat, or a drunkard's nose, of a cab or omnibus [see Plate 3.15, p. 65] – of a distant mountain with miles of atmosphere between it and the figures in the foreground.[19]

It was left to Layard to draw to a conclusion the different strands of this debate. He sums up the elements that made Keene's work amusing to the casual reader and intensely interesting to the serious artist:

> Keene's humour was the humour of observation rather than the humour of invention. An acute observer of Nature, an eager spectator of the passing expressions and moods of his fellow-creatures, an impressionist of the finest quality, given a subject which he could fully appreciate, and he would picture it with an unerring certainty, an uncompromising realism.[20]

NOTES

1. Fitzwilliam MSS 34, Keene.
2. Reid, 1928, p. 119.
3. Layard, 1892, p. 351.
4. ibid., p. 180.
5. ibid., p. 186.
6. ibid., p. 188.
7. Private Collection.
8. Burnand, 1904, p. 11.
9. Layard, 1892, p. 193.
10. ibid., p. 198.
11. Private Collection.
12. Layard, 1907, p. 177.
13. Layard, 1892, p. 203.
14. Du Maurier, 1898, p. 104.
15. ibid., p. 104.
16. ibid., pp. 82–83.
17. Pennell, 1897b, p. 13.
18. Layard, 1892, p. 204.
19. Du Maurier, 1898, pp. 88–89.
20. Layard, 1892, p. 204.

5 Keene and the world of art

Keene's reputation as a bohemian and a loner, tended to be somewhat exaggerated by his contemporaries, particularly by those of the *Punch* table. F.G. Burnand referred in his memoirs to Keene as 'a kind of hermit artist, living in a style that suited him, but which I shall say could never, by any possibility whatever have suited anybody else'.[1] In his diary for 1872 Shirley Brooks records that Keene 'works in a house with 3 other artists, and they have no servant, but an old "char" cleans them out – very little I daresay'.[2] This was No. 11 Queen's Road, West, Chelsea, where he lived with F. Wilfred Lawson for seven years. Such tales added to the artist's eccentric image and even to the suggestion that he was dirty. An unkind advertisement for soap by Harry Furniss, was supposed to have been a portrait of Keene and caused the wretched man great offence. In reality, Keene was quite sociable on his own terms, was cleanly if simply dressed and set great store by having his boots made in the West End. He certainly needed good footwear as he walked miles back and forth to Chelsea with his rather rolling gait. A Chelsea maid noticing this commented, 'Mr Keene do walk like a lord!'

Shirley Brooks' diary equally bears witness to Keene's social side. He notes on 19 June 1869 that Keene attended a party at the German Reeds for an entertainment and play, the company including Colonel de Bathe, Mark Lemon, Val Prinsep, Mr Macmillan, the Millais, Tenniel, Cruikshank, Arthur Sullivan, Linley Sambourne, Alfred Elmore and most of Victorian artistic society. He was also to be found at smart dinner parties given by Luke Fildes, R.A., one at Melbury Road in 1886 included the Americans J.S. Sargent and Edwin Austin Abbey and the British painter Frank Holl. At the Queen's Gate mansion of J.P. Heseltine, he might meet the leading architects of the day and William Morris.

Keene's close-knit family circle at the White Cottage had not encouraged him to move far from the parental roof. His attachment to his mother and sisters was intense; they were his constant models and companions, and though this fireside was diminished by the marriages of his brother and one sister, it remained the great anchor of his life. But even they could not control his hankering after the countryside and it was this longing to be in the open fields that led to an important development in 1865.

5.1   Charles Keene by J. D. Watson (1832–1892).
      Pen and sepia ink.   6 x 4in.   15 x 12cm.
      Peter Nahum Ltd.

Keene's friend and fellow illustrator Birket Foster (1825–99) had settled on an estate at Witley in Surrey where he had built himself an ample residence, The Hill. He was an immensely successful artist and wished to gather round him a colony of like-minded people for neighbours. In time this was to include his brother-in-law, the illustrator J.D. Watson (1832–92) and *his* brother-in-law, the collector J.P. Heseltine already mentioned. On his property, Foster had a small cottage, Tigbourne Cottage, where he had once resided and he offered this to Charles Keene to rent. Keene was delighted and wrote to a friend:

> This is a pleasant retreat to fly to for a day or two from the row and turmoil of London and gives my friends too the opportunity of calling it my 'country house,' and the pleasure of making me wince by hinting at the wealth that enables me to afford such a luxury! ... It's a bosky-copsey country, very picturesque and English, with just a suggestion (compared to Scotland) of hills on the horizon (the Hog's Back), but from there being so many trees, when the glass does fall the rain comes down with a vengeance.[3]

5.2   Photograph of Charles Keene in middle age.

He refers to the 'small aristocracy of artists' at Witley and mentions Foster, Burton, Watson and Jones and the festivities at The Hill when they dressed up in Elizabethan costume to perform masques and glees. Keene enjoyed this for a time, but in a letter to Mrs Edwards of early 1866 he writes 'we can keep "Les Autres Witleyites" at a distance.'[4]

The friendship with the Edwards had come a few years earlier. Edwin Edwards (1823–79) was a wealthy painter and etcher who had specialised in coast and river scenery. He had begun life as a successful lawyer in the Admiralty division of the courts but had given this up in 1860 to concentrate on the arts. His wife Elizabeth Ruth, an intelligent and elegant woman printed his etchings and entertained his friends at Thames Bank House, Sunbury. They often rented country houses for the summer and it was Keene who opened their eyes to the coast and estuaries around Southwold, Dunwich and Woodbridge, Suffolk. This resulted in them renting Cliff Cottage, Southwold for a number of years where he was a frequent guest.

More significantly from Keene's point of view, the Edwards had a wide acquaintance among Continental artists. They were close friends of Henri Fantin-Latour and Alphonse Legros, and were solely responsible for supplying Fantin with British commissions when his fortunes were at a low ebb. It is his double portrait of the couple in the Tate Gallery that remains their most lasting memorial today. They had taken in many French artist *émigrés* after the revolutions of 1870–71. They were also patrons of the painters Jacquemart and Jacques Emil Blanche and it may have been through them that Edgar Degas got to know Keene's work, for they had works by him and Legros on their walls.

It may have been Edwin Edwards' involvement with etching that rekindled for Keene the techniques he had learnt as an apprentice. He had etched a few plates before his meeting with Edwards in 1863, notably 'The Lee Shore' (1858) and 'Scene of the Plague', both for the publications of the Junior Etching Club. Edwards' rather moody and antiquarian work, such as his series of *Old Inns of England* would have greatly appealed to Keene's historical sense and he later refers to this series in his letters to Mrs Edwards.

Keene's etchings form a fairly small group, but as they relate so closely to his drawings and other work, they must be dealt with here. They number 34 plates if we exclude the *Punch* 'Pocket Book' frontispieces and two disputed items. They represent the artist in his most relaxed form, carrying out the work that he most wanted to do on holiday in Surrey or Suffolk. There is no deadline here, no sign of that pressure to please his bosses at the magazine, just straight unalloyed pleasure. This accounts for the subjects being taken at random, having no theme and in some cases being uncompleted.

It has to be remembered that an etching revival was under way in the 1860s, and that Keene's friend Whistler was very much a part of it. Whistler had

5.3   J. E. Millais by Charles Keene, *c.* 1865.
Pen and ink, Studio stamp.   6 x 3¹/₂in.   15 x 19cm.
Michael Broadbent Collection.

published an etching alongside Keene in the Junior Etching Club volume of *Passages From Modern English Poets* in 1862, a comparatively rare example of his book illustration. The two artists were closest at this time, when Whistler was just beginning his career and Keene was already established. It was a strange friendship, the fastidious dandy Whistler and the bohemian Keene, but probably the former realised that Keene was not a social rival and could afford to be generous about his abilities as a draughtsman.

5.4   Mrs Edwin Edwards, late 1860s.
Pen and black ink.   3 × 4in.   9 × 12.5cm.
The Syndics of The Fitzwilliam Museum.

5.5 Edwin Edwards (1823–1879).
Etching.   4³/₄ × 3¹/₄in.   12 × 8cm.
Michael Broadbent Collection.

5.6 Portrait of Madame Zambaco sketching.
Etching.   16.5 × 10cm.
Michael Broadbent Collection.

5.7   Lady of 1860 seated, probably Miss Keene.
Etching.   6 × 5in.   15 × 13cm.
Michael Broadbent Collection.

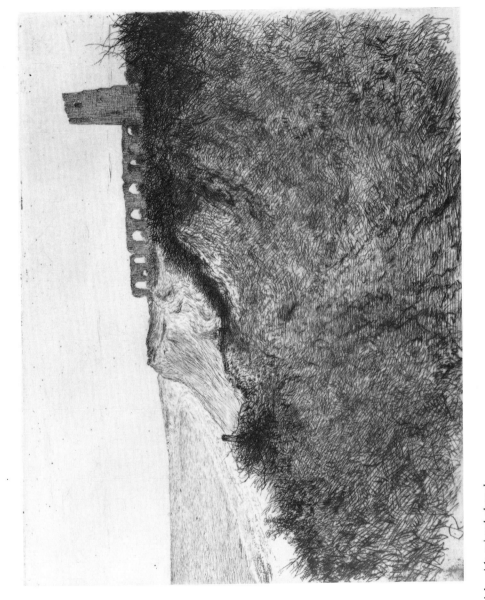

5.8 Dunwich with ruined church.
Etching. 2 × 7¼in. 5.5 × 18.5cm.
Michael Broadbent Collection.

91

5.9   Elderly man seated in an armchair.
Etching.   6 x 5in.   15 x 13cm.
Michael Broadbent Collection.

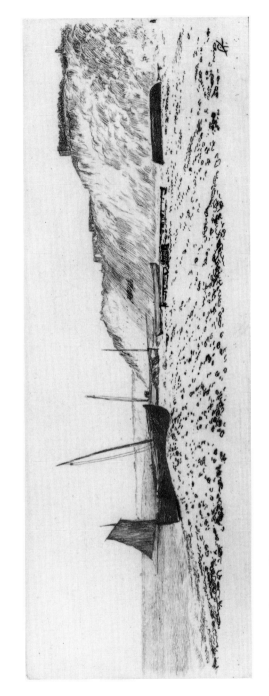

5.10   Coast scene, Seaton, Devon.
Etching.   4 x 6in.   10 x 17.5cm.
Michael Broadbent Collection.

5.11   Canal scene, Watford.
Etching.   6 x 3³/₄in.
Michael Broadbent Collection.

The artists come closest together in the etched line and it is interesting that both focused on rivers and seascapes and both lived close to one another. Perhaps the nearest approximation is in Keene's 'Southwold Harbour', a superb tonal plate with a tiny glimpse of the sea in the distance and a wonderful foreground of shining shingle surrounded by weather-beaten wood. Similarly rich effects can be seen in Whistler's 'Lion Wharf' but the American artist's foregrounds are more nervously impressionistic. There are striking similarities too in the figure subjects, Keene's 'Lady Reading a Book' makes play with patches of light and shade in the model's full skirt much as Whistler does in the skirt and bodice of his 'Finette'. Although Keene's etched work is undated, it is presumed that the girl reading is 1859–60 (see Plate 5.7, p. 90), probably within months of Whistler's work. There is also a parallel in the way Keene conceives his 'Cambridge Grisette' and Whistler his 'Annie Hayden', both encasing the innocence and charm of the subject in an almost sculptural form.

It was a compliment to Keene's gentleness and stature that his friendship with Whistler survived the year 1878. This was the time when the celebrated Whistler vs. Ruskin trial took place in London and the American artist asked Keene to give evidence in his defence. 'Whistler's case against Ruskin comes off, I believe, on Monday,' Keene wrote to a friend,

> He wants to subpoena me as a witness as to whether he is (as Ruskin says) an impostor or not. I told him I should be glad to record my opinion but begged him to do without me if he could. They say it will be most likely settled on the point of law without going into evidence, but if the evidence is adduced, it will be the greatest lark that has been known for a long time in the courts.[5]

Perhaps Whistler recognised that Keene's self-effacing nature would have made such an action impossible. He certainly retained the friendship and when Whistler was president of the British Artists in 1886–88, he persuaded Keene to join and to leave with him at the end of his term.

Apart from a few costume studies, Keene's etchings tend to be intimate glimpses into the artist's private life, the houses that he inhabited, the countryside that he loved and the people with whom he felt most at home. We have views of the much-loved Tigbourne Cottage, upward glances at the landing in Birket Foster's house, the canal at Watford (see Plate 5.11, p. 94) and the rather gaunt toothless silhouette of the church at Dunwich (see Plate 5.8, p. 91). Perhaps the most successful however are the portraits of his close friends and their life, the interior of the Edwards house at Sunbury with Mrs Edwards painting, the concentrated figure of Edwin Edwards reading in his garden chair (see Plate 5.5, p. 89) or Madame Zambaco caught in the act of drawing as seen through a doorway (see Plate 5.6, p. 89). For Keene, Mr and Mrs Edwards became 'The Master' and 'The Mistress' and he was also a great admirer of the artistic Greek beauty Mary Zambaco and was said to particularly delight in her black hair! There is a fine etched portrait of Mrs J.P. Heseltine and the 'Lady Reading' of 1859–60 is believed to be a portrait of Miss Keene (see Plate 5.7, p. 90).

This is not to suggest that the subjects for Keene's etched work were exclusively drawn from his intimate circle – there are several plates that are clearly derived from Langham studies and some from his models. He made two etchings of a bad-tempered man, certainly a model, one of him seated in a chair with a scowl on his face (see Plate 5.9, p. 92) and another of him standing in a top hat and long frock coat. This was obviously posed in the artist's studio where Keene's ubiquitous stove and kettle can be seen in the background. Apart from the Junior Etching Club plates, the only etching to be published in his lifetime was 'Southwold Harbour' which appeared in *The Etcher* for 1881. The artist was notoriously careless about documenting these works and not even bothered about printing them. Fortunately he delegated this task to Mrs Edwards whom Layard described as one of the best printers in London.[6]

It was quite late in his life that Keene, through Henry Silver, met and became a friend of the great poet and translator Edward Fitzgerald (1809–83). Fitzgerald was an East Anglian like Keene and also an amateur artist and critic of the arts, but it must have been a love of music, literature and history that brought them together. Fitzgerald, who did not suffer fools gladly, at once recognised Keene's scholarship and sent him books that he found too difficult! In a letter to F.A. Wright in August 1880, Fitzgerald notes, 'Little must the readers of Punch know what a queer Spirit lurks behind those Woodcuts of his.'[7] The ancient poet and the not-so-ancient artist drank whiskey together and read Froissart and ancient books, as, Fitzgerald commented, neither were interested in anything modern. Keene came to calling Fitzgerald 'The Literate' in the way he had of giving names to everybody. On occasion Keene would bring down his bagpipes to play to Fitzgerald who writes in a letter of 1882, 'Keene has a theory that we open our mouths too much, but whether he bottles up his wind to play the bagpipes, or whether he plays the bagpipes to get rid of his bottled-up wind, I do not know.'

If the Edwards had given Keene access to French painters, it was to the German School that he had looked for inspiration. As a young man he had been fascinated by the work of Adolph Menzel (1815–1905) whose *Frederick the Great* he had actually owned. It was not until the 1880s that Menzel saw some of Keene's drawings in Berlin and showed a mutual interest in them. Menzel sent him a signed photograph at which the old bohemian was charmed and embarrassed. He told a friend, 'I'm thinking of sending him a few scraps of studies, if I can screw up my confidence, but I shall be in a funk when they are gone, I know.'[8] It seems likely that J.P. Heseltine was the go-between as it was he that reported on Menzel's delight with them. As a result of this exchange of work, Menzel became a subscriber to *Punch* purely so that he could enjoy Keene's work. Probably the only place Keene would have seen original Menzel sketches previously would have been in the cabinets of his friend J.P. Heseltine at Queen's Gate.

It is not difficult to see why Keene had so great an admiration for the German illustrator. The strength of his line work and the precision of his detail, particularly in pencil, ranked with the highest nineteenth-century work. Menzel was more of a watercolourist than Keene, but even here there is a similarity in their approach, both preferring the painterly use of washes to the careful application of most Victorians.

Keene felt that Menzel was very much 'in the track' of another German master, Daniel N. Chodowiecki (1726–1801). His admiration for this 'little master' as he called him was unbounded; he collected every print that he could lay his hands on and obviously tried to emulate the delicacy of the line and the fine tones evident

5.12 Barrister, *c.* 1879.
   Pencil and watercolour.   5¼ x 3¾in.   13.5 x 9.5cm.
   Michael Broadbent.

5.13   Lord Suffield. *c*. 1879.
Pen, ink and wash.   7 x 8³/₄in.   20 x 21cm.
The Visitors of The Ashmolean Museum.

in that artist's work. Chodowiecki was a prolific book illustrator at the end of the eighteenth century and drew for German calendars as well as for classics such as Shakespeare's plays, Goldsmith's *Vicar of Wakefield*, Sternes' *Tristram Shandy*, and Smollett's *Peregrine Pickle* and *Roderick Random*. He particularly liked Chodowiecki's illustrations to Richardson's *Clarissa Harlowe* and told Crawhall, 'I feel terribly tempted to sacrifice the book and cut 'em out. Do you know this artist's works? I consider him the most extraordinary demon of industry (and very excellent art of its sort) I ever knew of.'⁹ Again it does not seem likely that Keene

5.14 Robert from 'The Diary of a City Waiter', 1885.
Pen and ink.　　4 × 5³/₄in.　　10.3 x 14.5cm.
Michael Cook Collection.

5.15 Early Neglect, *c.* 1870.
Pencil and watercolour.　　5 × 4in.
Chris Beetles, St James's Ltd.

would have seen any original drawings in London, but Chodowiecki's studies are admirable and have the soft qualities found in the studies of the French artist Fragonard.

Among the English artists his passion was always for the wood engravings of Thomas Bewick. This was an enthusiasm increased by his friendship with North Country men like Crawhall and Barnes and the fact that George Price Boyce was a Bewick collector. Keene owned Bewick's walking-stick, a number of his lithographs and made a special pilgrimage in 1881 to see the artist's daughter, being rewarded with a rare proof of her father's.

Keene's work became known to some of the Impressionists on the other side of the Channel from the 1870s. When Lucien Pissarro decided to come to England, Camille Pissarro recommended the work of Keene to him as the major, almost the sole, contribution of Britain to the arts! 'England has Keene,' Pissarro wrote on 16 June 1883, 'he does not exhibit, he is not fashionable, and that is everything.'[10] With similar enthusiasm Edgar Degas had acquired a copy of Keene's collected works *Our People*.[11] When Degas' collection was sold on 6–7 November 1918, it included 215 Keene wood engravings that made 11 francs. Walter Sickert who knew many of the Impressionists better than any other English artist had these comments to make on Keene whom he must have known:

> Keene … for a three-penny weekly made drawings that are on a level with the finest in the world. Keene was the first of the moderns. He saw things never seen before. He observed the reflected lights in shadows and expressed them by lines drawn in diluted ink. The Impressionist painters were great admirers and students of his work. The painting of trees in sunlight by Monet and Sisley is based on his drawings. Keene's influence on these painters was stronger than Constable's.[12]

It was the energetic Mrs Edwards who first brought Keene to the notice of Continental critics, suggesting that he should be included by M. Beraldi in his *Les graveurs du dix-neuvième siècle* (1888). He wrote to Mrs Edwards:

> I have only scratched a few studies of sketches, not more than a dozen all told, I should think – the merest experiments! Titles they have not. To save my life I couldn't tell the dates – and as to writing my life Story! God bless you, sir, I've none to tell.[13]

Beraldi wrote:

> Keene, homme modeste, est de ceux que la critique met du temps a découvrir. Certes les artistes anglais l'apprécient, mais son nom n'est pas crié sur les toits comme celui de certains modernistes de bien moindre valeur.[14]

It was largely due again to Mrs Edwards' championing of her friend that Keene was honoured at the Paris International Exhibition of 1889. He certainly would never have been persuaded by anybody else to submit examples of his work to this show in which he espoused little enthusiasm. He was awarded the Gold Medal in September and wrote laconically to Crawhall,

That award from Paris was rather a surprise to me, as I had forgotten I had anything there. I did not send anything myself, but my friend Mrs Edwards contributed some. – It is a queer arrangement. They send you a cast, gilt I believe, and if you wish for the gold medal (proper) you can buy it for a price! I don't think I shall invest![15]

To J. Sands he commented, 'I've not seen it in my newspapers & I've had no official notice.'[16] He never appears to have acquired the Gold Medal, being content with the engraved Diplôme de Médaille hung in an oak frame!

From the early 1880s, Keene's circle of friends began to contract. He had already lost the use of Tigbourne Cottage in 1876, due to a calculating friend usurping the lease, resulting in one of the few quarrels he ever had. Edwin Edwards had died in 1879, and he was followed in May 1881 by Mrs Mary Keene, the mother who had developed a very special relationship with her son. 'My poor old mother is on her death-bed,' he wrote to a friend the month before, … Her look and the tones of her voice "go to the marrow of my bones", and knock me over very much.'[17] The next to depart was Edward Fitzgerald 'The Literate' whom Keene had come to rely on for antiquarian talk on the Suffolk coast. In an undated letter to Sir Henry Thompson, Whistler's friend, Keene wrote:

I'm a book lover & collect & read everything I can find about our Eastern Counties & folk. I used to enjoy my fill of this love when staying with poor Fitzgerald of Woodbridge I dare say you knew him. He was a bookworm too & charming talker & a great pleasure of my life was gone when he died, I've not been there since.[18]

Perhaps the greatest shock was the death of his sister Kate Keene in March 1884, a dearly loved companion whose figure he had modelled from so many times.

If Keene's own friends were slipping away, he was at least keeping in touch with a new generation of artists. He was intensely interested in Joseph Crawhall's son, Joseph Crawhall, jun. (1860–1913), who was to become an outstanding painter in the group known as the Glasgow Boys. The younger Crawhall was to make his name as a painter of animals and birds in a slick post-Impressionist manner reflecting his Paris training. Keene would have appreciated the treatment of light and the economy of brushstrokes in these works. Writing to the father in July 1880 he enquires:

How does Joe get on with his painting? That disposition he seems to have of getting dissatisfied with his work shows he's a real artist, but try and get him to stick hard to his ideas and work 'em out to the bitter end! – the end will perhaps be bitter for some time, but it must be swallowed.[19]

Later in 1889 he says, 'It was interesting but tantalising the account of Joe's works in the paper you sent me, I wish he'd send some to London that we could see them.'[20] Keene continued to show a great interest in the young man and whether he was exhibiting at the Royal Academy.

In the same letter Keene remarks on a new journal that he has seen in London:

I quite agree with you about the 'Hobby Horse' a little of it goes a great way – I notice some new disciples in the aesthetic line, some examples of which appear in 'Arry Quilter's magazine (forget the name – crimson cover) & I see the same artists are bringing out a new organ 'The Dial' have you seen it? Very Blakey & mysterious![21]

Here we have Keene commenting not unenthusiastically on the next generation of illustrators: Arthur Mackmurdo, Selwyn Image, Charles Ricketts and Charles Shannon.

Keene's vast accumulation of props for the artist which had followed him around from the Strand to Langham Chambers and then Queen's Road, West, had finally in 1879 come to rest at 283 King's Road, Chelsea. There it was constantly in demand by other artist friends, Luke Fildes borrowing a traditional countryman's smock for one of his pictures and most of his visitors commenting on the array of things. Keene was followed everywhere by his favourite dachshunds which he regularly took to Surrey to have mated. He was most unhappy in the early 1880s to be summoned by the magistrates for not having a dog licence, an act he put down to a malicious neighbour.

As early as 1865, Keene had complained of lumbago in a letter to Mrs Edwards, 'the result of damp knifeboards' that is, riding on omnibuses.[22] In 1878 he was suffering from rheumatism in his hands, a worrying complaint for any artist, and by the mid-1880s he was constantly unwell. It is hardly surprising that a man of over sixty who did not look after himself and ate a punishing diet of meals at random times should suffer from stomach trouble. He had heartburn and became exhausted after walking more than 500 yards, part of which could be laid at the door of his old friend tobacco. Even in 1876 he was advising his ailing friend Edwards to go on smoking: 'I think after a time, a certain amount, rigidly not exceeded would be beneficial to you.'[23]

The only bright star in the sky was Crawhall, who still kept up his correspondence and announced that he was moving to London in 1890. But by August 1889, Keene appreciated that he was too ill to go on alone in his lodgings and would have to move in with his surviving sister and her servant. He wrote sadly to Crawhall:

> I've begun to make a clearance of Chelsea, summoned a man I've known a long time Model & Window Cleaner who brought a truck which was soon filled up, old clothes, a sack of boots, shoes, furniture, drawing-boards, books, countless folios of prints, that I used to collect when a boy! since then have sold 5 chairs & 2 oak chests, there will be some things left till the last that will be hard to part with, a Dummy horse and saddle, Pier glass, &c that I've not room for in this small House – and every day it seems clearer to me my days of working in a studio are over!

A month later he comments, ' ... I'm busy burning, destroying & dispersing & packing up the dusty accumulations of years at Chelsea & a fatiguing & painful work.'[24]

Keene's last *Punch* drawing had appeared on 16 August 1890, after that he was in too much pain to contribute. During that summer the art establishment paid

5.16 Beware. An Aesthetic Couple. *Punch*, 10 March 1883.
Pen and ink.   7 × 4¹/₂in.
Chris Beetles, St James's Ltd.

5.17 Our Failures. *Punch*, 3 February 1877.
Pen and ink with Studio stamp.   5 × 4in.
Chris Beetles, St James's Ltd.

5.18   Popular Fallacies. *Punch*, 4 August 1883.
        Pen and ink and bodycolour.   5¹/₄ × 4¹/₄in.
        Chris Beetles, St James's Ltd.

5.19   Self-Portrait. 1870s.
        Pen and ink.   10 × 6in.
        Chris Beetles, St James's Ltd.

their respects in person, William Holman Hunt, Sir John Millais and many of his *Punch* colleagues, all aware that it was only a question of time. F.G. Burnand had noted the gradual change over the years:

> When I first met Charles Keene in the old days at young Buckstone's and Matt Morgan's studio, with Millais, Prinsep, Leighton, Marcus Stone, 'Dolly' Storey, and *toute la boutique artistique* of that period, he was very different from the Charles Keene of the later days. Perhaps he overtaxed his physical strength, and did not take in enough fuel to keep the engine-fires going.[25]

Strangely enough he had developed a great dislike of tobacco in the last year. He had confided to a friend:

> … the doctors pronounced my case one of intense dyspepsia, that had been coming on for some time, when it culminated about three months ago. I suddenly took a horror of tobacco, and the taste has not returned since; I wish it would, and then I should be reassured I was getting better.[26]

But the case was obviously more serious, the swollen feet and breathlessness perhaps pointing to heart disease. In a letter to his friend Barnes in December 1889, he had described himself as 'so woefully lean, in my "buff" I'm like one of Albert Durer's Anatomies …'[27]

Another plague was sent to try him at the extreme end of his life: journalistic interviews. Most Victorians hated any intrusion into their private lives and the new fashion from America of interviewing celebrities was much resented. An attempt by Raymond Blathwayt to interview Keene for the *Pall Mall Gazette* failed in November 1889. The artist wrote confidentially to Barnes on 17 December:

> You said in your letter about that snobbish interviewing business that has been going on in the 'Pall Mall' … I did not so much wonder at Sambourne who is a little artless Philistine, but I was surprised at du Maurier's falling in with it, I enclose the snob's cheeky note, observe he evidently thinks I should jump at it, I choked him off as politely as I could but this was difficult.[28]

In a particularly sad letter to Barnes he rather uncharacteristically complains of his ailments and his treatment by *Punch*. 'My small troubles have increased and multiplied,' he writes in May 1890,

> my feet and ankles have swelled & I have to keep them up, this prevents me from doing work even if I felt inclined, which *I do not*. The Editor has no sympathy with my work & shelves my drawings so that I don't get paid for them & I'm getting altogether out of touch with the Staff, though they wrote very kindly refusing my resignation. If you had seen me last Saturday when I was in uneasy pain & a sleepless night therefrom, & though free from acute pain on Sunday & Monday yet unable to move or be moved without yelling, you would not have thought me a cheerful inmate of your pleasant home.[29]

Fortunately Joseph Crawhall was now established in Ealing and able to visit his friend in the mornings to cheer him up.

The great draughtsman just survived into the decade of the 1890s, the golden period of black and white draughtsmanship, but died on 4 January 1891. He was laid to rest in Hammersmith cemetery attended by all his *Punch* friends. His will was extremely short and simple; they found he did not describe himself as artist but 'gentleman' and that most of the terms were concerned with an annuity to his servant Mary Ann Smith. Friends were astonished that he had left nearly thirty thousand pounds, a sum achieved not through frugality but by hard work and an uncomplicated style of life. Most of his acquaintances were aware of his ascetic approach to everything that did not involve his art. Forty years later, Edith Hipkins recalled:

> He loathed 'waste' and 'tips' vexed him – for economy ruled his life from start to finish. Not that he was mean – far from it – for to his friends he was generosity itself; but no medieval monk ever lived a more austere life (save in buying fine books!). Every scrap of un-used letter-paper, the interiors of envelopes, even the flaps, were of use to him – the very lamp-shade in his home was carefully patched with the adhesive edging of postage stamps. When at home, the hearth rug was rolled up and placed out of harm's way beneath the table.[30]

It fell to Mrs Edwin Edwards to dispose of things to his friends, a lock of his hair that she herself had cut, a silver spoon that had belonged to Thomas Bewick, treasured examples of etchings and drawings. Perhaps it was she who arranged the retrospective exhibition at the Fine Art Society the following spring. One wonders exactly what the relationship was between the artist and this intelligent woman who was his chief correspondent for 20 years: confidante, companion or something more? Keene's legacy to the art world was even harder to define. He left no pupils and he had certainly not established a school. At the Academy Banquet of 1891 (an event that Keene had occasionally attended) Lord Leighton praised him:

> Never have the humours of the life of certain classes of Englishmen been seized with such unerring grasp as in his works; never have they been arrested with a more masterly, artistic skill. Among the documents for the study of future days of middle-class and of humble English life, none will be more weighty than the vivid sketches of this great humourist.[31]

Foreign journals in particular paid glowing tributes after his death, notably the French ones *L'Artiste, La Chronique des Arts* and *Art Moderne*. But perhaps the greatest tribute came from artists themselves who continued to talk about his work and collect it for their own walls.

We have already mentioned Whistler's statement to Pennell that he was 'the greatest artist since Hogarth'. Phil May paid him a fulsome tribute by saying 'he's the daddy of the lot of us!' Keene was referred to as 'the artist's artist' and it is true that of the eight books published about Keene, three of them have been by artists: Joseph Pennell, the illustrator, Lionel Lindsay, the distinguished Australian etcher and F.L. Emanuel, topographer and draughtsman. One can well understand why there should be this empathy. Lionel Lindsay wrote,

> Such a style never was, never could be, popular with the general public. As well ask Suburbia to comprehend the *baigneuses* of Degas, or the swift drawings of Rembrandt. The largeness of Keene's vision, the breadth and simplicity of his handling, could best be enjoyed by those truly educated in art matters.[32]

The artists who collected Keene's work are equally significant. Charles Ricketts and Charles Shannon had twelve Keenes in their great collection – these are now at Cambridge. Both the *Punch* illustrator Leonard Raven Hill and the artist Charles Fairfax Murray were enthusiasts. Sir Frank Brangwyn had a Keene on the wall of his house and Sir Alfred Munnings presented one to his old school. In the 1930s, Duncan Grant had one fastened to the wall of his studio at Charlston Farm and both Thomas Lowinsky and Eliot Hodgkin had examples in their collections.

Perhaps therefore the last word should be left to an artist, Lionel Lindsay:

> Master of form and every effect of weather, the suggestion of the movement of wind and water, of ships and horses, came as easily to his hand as did spring light on English fields and woods, the tone and character of Scottish hills and moors, or London's grey. He sophisticated nothing, and because of this one need never be in doubt about an unsigned Keene drawing, for, apart from the personality of touch, there is always present in his slightest sketch a way of seeing and summarising a form that distinguishes his work from every other artist.[33]

Notes

1. Burnand, 1904, p. 11.
2. Layard, 1907, p. 524.
3. Layard, 1892, p. 102.
4. Fitzwilliam MSS 12, Keene.
5. Pennell, 1908, p. 168.
6. Layard, 1892, p. 107.
7. Terhune, 1980, p. 356.
8. Layard, 1892, p. 56.
9. ibid., p. 155.
10. Rewald, 1944, p. 35.
11. Reff, p. 5.
12. Emmons, 1941, p. 245.
13. Layard, 1892, p. 38.
14. Beraldi, Vol 8, p. 283.
15. Layard, 1892, p. 410.
16. Private Collection.
17. Layard, 1892, p. 315.
18. Author's Collection.
19. Layard, 1892, p. 311.
20. Private Collection.
21. ibid.
22. Fitzwilliam MSS 30, Keene.
23. ibid., 56.
24. Private Collection.
25. Burnand, 1904, p. 11.
26. Layard, 1892, p. 406.
27. Private Collection.
28. Private Collection. His antipathy to Sambourne may have been mutual. In 1892 Sambourne was given a Keene sketch which he promptly gave to Burnand.
29. Private Collection.

30. Lindsay, 1934, p. 131.
31. Layard, 1892, p. 440.
32. Lindsay, 1934, p. 91.
33. ibid., p. 8.

Bibliography

Alphabet and Image, No 8, 'The last days of Charles Keene', 1948. 4to, 100 pp.

Anon., 'Charles Keene,' *Pall Mall Magazine*, October 1908.

Arts Council, *Drawings by Charles Keene*, 1952, catalogue. Introduction by Sir Kenneth Clark.

Beraldi, Henri, *Les Gravures du XIX Siècle*, 1888, Vol 8, p. 283.

Burnand, Sir F.G., *Records and Reminiscences*, 2 vols, Methuen 1904. 8vo, i–xix, 424pp, xx–xxxviii, 464 pp.

Cohen, J.M., ed., *The Letters of Edward Fitzgerald*, Centaur Press, 1960. 8vo, 276 pp.

Du Maurier, Daphne, *The Young George du Maurier*, Peter Davies, 1951. 8vo, i–xxi, 307 pp.

Du Maurier, George, *Social Pictorial Satire*, 1898.

Emanuel, Frank L., *Charles Keene, Etcher, Draughtsman and Illustrator 1823–1891*, being a Lecture delivered to the Print Collectors' Club on Friday, November 25th, 1932 ... 8vo, 72 pp.

Emmons, Robert, *The Life and Opinions of Walter Richard Sickert*, Faber & Faber, 1942. 8vo, i–xii, 327 pp.

Engen, Rodney, *Dictionary of Victorian Wood-Engravers*, 1985, Cambridge, Chadwyck-Healey.

—— *Sir John Tenniel: Alice's White Knight*, Scolar Press, 1991.

Fine Art Society, *Catalogue of the Work of Charles Keene*, 1891.

Gray, Basil, *The English Print*, Adam & Charles Black, 1927. 8vo, 266 pp.

Hone, Joseph, *The Life of Henry Tonks*, Heinemann, 1939. 8vo, 390 pp.

Houfe, Simon, *Charles Keene*, (Essays and catalogue) Christie's exhibition, 1991.

Hudson, Derek, *Charles Keene*, London, Pleaides Books, MCMXLVII. 4to, 56 pp.

Layard, George Somes, *The Life and Letters of Charles Keene*, London, Sampson Lowe, 1892. 4to, xxi + 463 pp.

—— *Shirley Brooks, Great Punch Editor*, 1907.

Leicester Galleries, *Catalogue of an exhibition of Drawings by Charles Keene 1832–1891*, 1966.

Lindsay, Sir Lionel, *Charles Keene The Artist's Artist*, P. & D. Colnaghi (Limited

Edition) 1934.

Lowinsky Collection. ... *Catalogue of Drawings By Charles Keene*, Leicester Galleries, 1952.

Muir, Percy, *Victorian Illustrated Books*, Batsford, 1971 and 1985. 8vo, i–ix, 287 pp.

Pennell, Joseph, *Pen Drawing and Pen Draughtsmen their Work and their Methods a Study of The Art Today with Technical Suggestions.* 4to, 462 pp.

—— *The Work of Charles Keene with an Introduction & Comments on the Drawings Illustrating the Artist's Methods,* ... Bibliography of the Books Illustrated and a Catalogue of his Etchings by W.H. Chesson. T. Fisher Unwin, Bradbury, Agnew & Co Ltd, London, MDCCCXCVII. Folio. Photogravure frontispiece + 289 pp.

—— *Modern Illustration*, George Bell, London and New York, MDCCCXCV. 8vo, 146 pp.

—— and Pennell, Elizabeth R., *The Life of James McNeil Whistler*, Heinemann, 1908. 8vo, 450 pp.

Piper, Myfanwy, *Charles Keene*, Signature, 1952. 4to, 54 pp.

Print Collector's Quarterly, Forrest Reid 'Charles Keene Illustrator' No. 17, 1930 pp. 23–47.

Ray, Gordon N., *The Illustrator And The Book in England From 1790 To 1914*, Pierpont Morgan, 1976. 4to, 336 pp.

Reff, Theodore Franklin *Degas Notebooks*, 2 Vols, 1976, Clarendon Press, Oxford.

Reid, Forrest, *Illustrators of The Sixties*, Faber & Gwyer, 1928. 4to, 296 pp.

Reitlinger, Henry, *From Hogarth to Keene*, Methuen & Co Ltd, 1938. 8vo, i–xii, 115 pp.

Rewald, John, *Camille Pissarro, Letters to his son Lucien*, 1944.

Ritchie, M.T., ed., *English Drawings Number ten (Charles Samuel Keene)*, Chatto & Windus 1935, 4to, 96 pp.

Rothenstein, William, *Men and Memories* Recollections of ... Faber & Faber, 1932.

Spectator, The, W.M. Rossetti, 'The Art of Punch', 21 September 1861, pp. 1035–1036.

Spielmann, M.H., *The History of Punch*, Cassell & Co, 1895. 4to, 592 pp.

—— *Twenty-One Etchings By Charles Keene*, With an Introduction by ... The Astolar Press, 1903. Portfolio.

Stacy Marks, Henry, *Pen and Pencil Sketches*, 2 Vols, Chatto & Windus, 1894. 8vo, i–xix, 263 pp.; i–xiii, 259 pp.

Terhune, A. & A., eds, *The Letters of Edward Fitzgerald*, 1980.

Index